# HEIRLOOM RECIPES

From

# The Spade and Trowel Garden club

Established 1927

Reorganized 2011

Published by
The Spade and Trowel
Garden Club,
Brevard County, Florida
September 2019

## ACKNOWLEDGEMENTS

Book and Cover design by William Serle
billserle.com

Cover Art courtesy of Sandy Starr
sandystarr.com

Computer entry by Carol Scott

Whimsical drawings by Sarah Smith

Dear Reader,

We are happy that you bought a copy of this Spade and Trowel cookbook.

Our club raises substantial sums every year at our annual Home Tour and other events. Funds come from the sale of tickets, the sale of crafts and baked goods and, now, from the sale of this book

*Heirloom Recipes* is the work of many people: the members who contributed recipes, Carol Scott who entered them into her computer, Sarah Smith who created the delightful little women to inhabit these pages, and William Serle, my husband, who formatted and printed it.

The club meets monthly and members take turns preparing food for the gatherings. Many dishes that made an appearance at meetings are now in this cookbook.

Spade and Trowel provides fellowship for the members and helps fund several local charities. Our principle beneficiaries at this time are Candlelighters (children with cancer), Walk on Water (A ministry of horse therapy for children with special needs) and Gabrielle's Place (Center for Women and Children).

*Daisy Serle*
President

# About Spade & Trowel Garden Club

The present club came into being in 2011. Its parent was the Cocoa-Rockledge Garden club (C-RGC). C-RGC was founded in 1927 and met in a variety of locations until moving into a purpose-built center constructed in 1964.

C-RGC reorganized into four circles in the early 1950s: Spade and Trowel, Green Thumb, Straw Hat and Sun and Sand. Dirt Daubers was added in 1982.

The circles reunified in 2011 and Spade and Trowel circle withdrew from the parent and became independent.

The idea behind the present Spade and Trowel Garden Club is that it is limited to 32 regular members. Social and educational meetings are held at members' homes.

Money is raised for local charities through sale of crafts and baked goods and at the annual Christmas Home Tour.

The spirit of friendship and charity are alive and well here.

# GENERAL TABLE OF CONTENTS

# Appetizers

# APPETIZERS
# TABLE OF CONTENTS

# Curry/Rum Raisin Ball
## Evelyn Fraley

## Ingredients

2 8-Ounce packages Cream Cheese
½ Cup Raisins (soaked in bourbon or rum)
1 Cup honey roasted peanuts
1 Teaspoon curry powder
¾ Cup scallion onion tops
1 Jar Cross and Blackwell mango chutney
(Not the hot one)
Crackers

## Directions

Mix everything except the chutney in a blender but don't make peanut butter.

Let set in fridge.

When ready to serve cover with mango chutney

Serve with five-grain harvest crackers or any other crackers you choose.

1

# Bacon and Cheddar Pinwheels
## Daisy Serle

## Ingredients

One Can crescent rolls or one 8-ounce can
of refrigerated dough sheets.
2 Tablespoons ranch dressing
¼ Cup or 4 slices bacon crisp and crumbled
½ Cup fine shredded cheddar cheese
¼ Cup chopped green onion

## Directions

Heat oven to 350.°

Unroll dough; separate into 2 long
rectangles.

Press each into 12x4-inch rectangle, firmly
pressing perforations to seal.

If using dough sheet: Unroll dough; cut
lengthwise into 2 long rectangles. Press each
into 12x4-inch rectangle.

Spread dressing over each rectangle to
edges.

Sprinkle each with bacon, cheddar cheese and onions.

Starting with one short side, roll up each rectangle; press edge to seal.

With serrated knife, cut each roll into 8 slices; place cut side down on ungreased cookie sheet.

Bake 12 to 17 minutes or until edges are deep golden brown. Immediately remove from cookie sheet.

Serve warm.

# Empanadas
## Carol Beebe

When I make these empanadas, I make the appetizer size, but they can be made much larger. I also make a double batch.

Make the meat filling the same day you are assembling empanadas, and not the day before.

MEAT FILLING:

## Ingredients

1 Package Chili-O Mix
½ Cup Tomato Paste
½ Cup green bell pepper chopped fine
½ Cup onion chopped fine
1 or 2 Hot peppers to taste, chopped fine. (I use Scotch Bonnets, but they can overpower, I urge caution and taste as you add)

## Directions

Brown meat first, drain excess fat.  Add all

other ingredients and cook until onion and peppers are opaque.

PASTRY:

The pasty must be made the night before and refrigerated for 12 hours. I use my hands to mix the ingredients ~ such fun!

## Ingredients

18 Ounces of Philly cream cheese.
(This does not come in a 9 oz package, so you combine packages)
1 Pound of butter
4 Cups flour
1 Teaspoon. salt
Evaporated Milk (not used in Pastry)

## Directions

Combine all ingredients except for milk. Work into a smooth ball, cover and refrigerate overnight.

Roll two hands full of pastry on floured surface until thin. If too thick, empanadas will be doughy. (Continued next page)

## EMPANADAS CONTINUED:

Use a regular drinking glass (2½-3" round) to stamp out circles of dough. Drop on to middle of each circle 1 tablespoon of the meat mixture.

Using fingertip, circle around edges of empanadas with water. This helps seal when crimped.

Fold dough over to form half circle over your meat mixture. Crimp along edges with fork which you have dipped into water to keep empanada sealed.

After sealing, using pastry brush, lightly brush top of empanada with evaporated milk.

Bake at 400° for 12-15 minutes or when golden brown.

Can be frozen for future use and keeps well in freezer bags. I do not recommend re-heating in microwave ovens.

# Zucchini Parmesan Crisps
## Daisy Serle
Crispy and addicting!

## Ingredients

½ Cup vegetable oil
1 Cup Panko (Japanese-style breadcrumbs)
½ Cup grated Parmesan cheese
2 Zucchinis thinly sliced to ¼ inch rounds
½ Cup all-purpose flour
2 Large eggs, beaten

## Directions

Heat vegetable oil in a large skillet over medium high heat.
In a large bowl, combine Panko and Parmesan; set aside.

Working in batches, dredge zucchini rounds in flour, dip into eggs, then dredge in Panko mixture, pressing to coat.
Add zucchini rounds to the skillet, 5 or 6 at a time, and cook until evenly golden and crispy, about a minute on each side.
Transfer to a paper towel-lined plate.
Serve immediately.

# Apple-Pecan Baked Brie
## Pat Bankhead

## Ingredients

1 Tablespoon butter
1 Small, tart, apple, peeled and sliced (I cut into small dices.)
$1/3$ Cup dried cranberries (Craisins) (Rough chopped)
¼ Cup chopped pecans
1 Tablespoon brown sugar
¼ Teaspoon ground cinnamon
Dash ground nutmeg
1 8-Ounce round Brie cheese
Assorted crackers

## Original directions

Preheat oven 375.°
In a saucepan, heat butter over medium heat.
Add apple, cranberries, pecans, brown sugar, cinnamon and nutmeg.
Cook and stir 5-7 minutes or until apple is tender.
Cut Brie horizontally in half. Place in a 9"
pie plate. Top with half of the apple mixture,

replace top and cover with the remaining apple mixture.

Bake uncovered 10-12 minutes or until cheese begins to melt.

Serve warm with crackers.

## My Directions

I did not follow the original instructions. I did cook the mixture in a saucepan, however, I just cut the white top off the Brie and microwaved it. Start with 20 seconds and add time as needed. After cheese comes out of the microwave top with the mixture from the saucepan.

Serve warm with crackers

# White Trash Snack Mix
## Linda Williams

One of my sisters makes this every year, usually around Christmas time, and it is hard to stay away from it. You can add your own version by adding M&M's or different cereals.

## Ingredients:

2 16-Ounce Packages White Almond Bark
1 Box of Golden Graham cereal
2 Cups salted peanuts (skinless)
1 16-Ounce bag mini pretzels

## Directions

Spread 18 inches of wax paper on your counter.
Fold all the ingredients, except the white almond bark, together in a large mixing bowl.
In a microwave-safe bowl, melt the almond bark in the microwave according to package directions.

Fold the melted almond bark into the cereal mixture until the mixture is evenly coated.

Pour out onto waxed paper and allow the bark to set.

Break up bark into pieces and serve.

Note: This will freeze well.
It makes a nice gift for different holidays.

Put pieces in an attractive bag and tie a ribbon around the top.

# Roquefort Cheese Balls
## Martha Chambers

## Ingredients

2 8-Ounce packages cream cheese
4 Ounces Roquefort or blue cheese
crumbled
1 Small jar Kraft Old English sharp cheese
1 Teaspoon Worcestershire sauce
¼ Medium onion chopped finely
1 Cup fresh chopped parsley
1 Cup chopped finely pecans

## Directions

Mix together the first 5 ingredients and half
of parsley and half of pecans.
Make two balls or 1 big one rolled in the
nuts mixed with parsley on waxed paper.
Refrigerate 3 hours.
Enjoy.

# Bongo Bongo Dip
## Rosemarie Galloway

A dip from 1970's college days

## Ingredients

8 Ounces softened cream cheese
1 Cup sour cream
8 Ounces cheddar cheese (reserve ½ ounce)
1 Envelope ranch salad dressing mix
10-Ounce package frozen chopped spinach
8-Ounce can water chestnuts
½ Cup chopped red pepper
¼ Cup chopped onions

## Directions

Preheat oven to 350º
Thaw spinach and drain well: set aside.
Mix all ingredients except reserved cheese.
Spray a casserole dish with cooking spray.
Pour ingredients into prepared pan.
Sprinkle reserved cheese on top.
Bake 25-30 minutes until bubbly.
Serve with French bread or garlic bread
slices.

# Blue Cheese Pecan Spread
## Daisy Serle

## Ingredient

½ Cup softened blue cheese
2 Tablespoons chopped, toasted pecans
Celery Stalks
Honey

## Directions

Mix cheese with chopped pecans
Spread on celery stalks
Drizzle with honey

# Onion Rings
## Bobbie Herlong

## Ingredients

Sliced onions
1 Cup flour
½ Cup beer
1 Egg plus 1 Egg white
1 Teaspoon baking powder
¾ Cup vegetable oil for frying

## Directions

Start by mixing ½ cup of flour with the beer.
Add the other ingredients to make a batter

Coat onions rings with mixture and fry in oil
at 350.º

# Beer Onion Rings
## Bobby Herlong

## Ingredients

Sliced onions
½ Cup Flour
½ Cup beer
Vegetable oil for frying

## Directions

Mix flour and beer. Dip Onion rings in
batter and Fry at 350.°

# Spinach Dip
## Betty Adamson

## Ingredients

8 Ounces softened cream cheese
1 Cup Sour Cream
1 Envelope Ranch Salad Dressing mix
1 9-Ounce package frozen Spinach – thawed
and well drained
1 8-Ounce can chopped water chestnuts
½ Cup chopped red pepper

## Directions

Mix all together. Serve with crackers

# Meatballs
## Betty Adamson

## Ingredients

MEATBALLS
2 Pounds ground beef
l Cup corn flake crumbs
1/3 Cup diced parsley flakes
2 Eggs – lightly beaten
2 Tablespoons soy sauce
¼ Teaspoon black pepper
½ Teaspoon garlic powder
1/3 cup catsup
2 Tablespoons dry onion flakes
Dash of salt
SAUCE
1 1-Pound can jellied cranberry sauce
l Bottle chili sauce
l Tablespoons brown sugar
1 Tablespoon lemon juice

## Directions

Combine meatball ingredients and mix well.
Make into, appetizer size meat balls.
Cook sauce until cranberry jelly softens.
Pour over meat balls. Bake 30 mins at 350.º

18

# Baked Chicken Fingers
## Bobbie Herlong

## Ingredients

1 Pound chicken tenders
2 Tablespoons honey
2 Tablespoons Mustard
2 Tablespoons buttermilk
½ Cup breadcrumbs
6 Tablespoons BBQ sauce or ranch dressing

## Directions

Whisk together honey, mustard and
buttermilk.
Coat chicken with mixture, then the
breadcrumbs.
Spray oil on baking sheet.
Place chicken fingers and bake 6 minutes at
450.°
Flip and cook 6 minutes more.

Serve BBQ sauce or ranch dressing on the
side.

# Appetizer Idea
## Bobbie Herlong

## Ingredients

Pitted dates filled with goat cheese and topped with bacon bits.

## Directions

Put into 350° oven for a few minutes.

# ENTREES

# ENTREES TABLE OF CONTENTS

# LE NOUVEAU MEAL PLAN
## Betty Fontana's Sister's Recipe

## Breakfast

1 Grapefruit
1 Slice whole wheat toast
1 Cup skim milk

## Lunch

1 Small portion lean, steamed chicken
1 Cup spinach
1 Cup herbal tea
1 Hershey's kiss

## Afternoon Tea

The rest of the Hershey Kisses in the bag.
1 tub of Hagen-Daaz ice cream with
chocolate chips.

(Continued next page)

## Dinner

4 Glasses of wine (red or white)
2 Loaves garlic bread
1 Family size supreme pizza
3 Snickers Bars

## Late Night Snack

1 Whole Sarah Lee cheesecake (eaten directly from the freezer)

Remember: Stressed spelled backward is desserts.

# Ham and Cheese Sliders
## Martha Chambers

## Ingredients

2 Dozen slider buns (I use rolls from Publix bakery)
2 Packages deli ham
2 Packages swiss cheese (I get large one)

SAUCE:
2 Sticks oleo
2 Tablespoons Worcestershire sauce
2 Tablespoons poppy seeds
4 Tablespoons brown sugar (I used 3 tablespoons of brown sugar)
2 Tablespoons yellow mustard

## Directions

Put ham and cheese in buns and place in two 9 x 13 pans.
Bring sauce ingredients to a boil and let cool
Pour over buns. Cover with foil and refrigerate overnight.
Cook covered for 25 minutes at 350,° then uncovered 5 minutes

# Beef and Biscuit Casserole
## Mary Jane Raleigh

## Ingredients

1¼ Pounds ground chuck
¼ Teaspoon garlic salt
½ Cup onion chopped
1 Can buttermilk biscuits
½ Cup chopped green pepper
2 Cups shredded medium cheddar cheese
2 Teaspoons chili powder
1 8-Ounce can tomato sauce
½ Cup sour cream
1 Egg slightly beaten

## Directions

Brown chuck, onion and pepper in frying pan.

Drain well.

Stir in tomato sauce, chili powder and garlic salt – simmer.

Separate biscuit dough into pieces (break at each line in dough) and press one layer into ungreased square pan.

Combine 2/3 cup cheese, sour cream and egg – mix well.

Remove meat mixture from pan and stir into sour cream mixture.
Spoon over dough in pan.

Arrange remaining biscuits on top, sprinkle with remaining cheese and bake at 375º for 25 minutes or until golden brown.

# Chicken Paprikash
## Monica Paige Sutton and Evelyn Fraley

## Ingredients

1 Onion chopped
2 Teaspoons salt
2 Tablespoons Shortening
1 ½ cup water
1 Tablespoon paprika
1 Chicken cut up
1 Teaspoon pepper
½ Pint sour cream

## Directions

Brown onion in shortening. Add seasonings and chicken. Brown 10 minutes.
Add water, cover and let simmer until done and tender.
Remove chicken, add sour cream and mix well. Put chicken back into sauce.
Make your favorite dumplings and add to chicken. Cook until the dumplings are done.
It's a good idea to double the sauce and, also, you can use half milk and half water.

# Reuben Casserole
## Carol Beebe

## Ingredients

6 Slices rye bread cubed and toasted
1 16-Ounce can Sauerkraut, drained and rinsed (I use the plastic packaged kraut in the dairy case)
1 Pound deli sliced corned beef (not wafer thin) cut into strips.
1 Cup Thousand island dressing
3 Cups shredded Swiss cheese

## Directions

Preheat oven to 400° – Spread bread cubes on the bottom of a 9x13-inch oiled baking dish.

Spread sauerkraut evenly over the bread cubes, then layer beef strips over sauerkraut.

Pour dressing over everything.

Spray aluminum foil with cooking spray and use to cover baking dish, sprayed side down. (Continued next page)

Bake in the preheated oven for 20 minutes.

Remove cover, sprinkle with cheese and bake uncovered for another 10 minutes, or until cheese is melted and bubbly.

Enjoy!

# Ravioli with Bacon and Tomato Cream
## Martha Chambers

The cream turns the flavors of bacon, onions and tomato into something magical. Everything you need to make this may already be in your fridge.

## Ingredients

8 Ounces cheese-filled ravioli
8 Slices bacon
4 Scallions, sliced thin
¼ Cup butter, cut into bits
2 Cups heavy cream
1 Cup freshly grated parmesan cheese
1 Cup peeled, seeded, chopped tomatoes
½ Teaspoon pepper, or to taste
¼ Teaspoon nutmeg, or to taste
½ Teaspoon salt, or to taste
Additional parmesan cheese

## Directions

Cook and drain ravioli
Fry bacon crisp. Drain on a paper towel.

(Continued next page)

Pour off all but 1 tablespoon fat from pan.

Add scallions to pan and cook over moderate heat, stirring for one minute.

Lift out to drain on paper towel. When bacon is cool, crumble it.

In a large saucepan cook butter and cream over moderate heat, stirring occasionally, for three minutes or until slightly thickened. Stir in the parmesan, crumbled bacon, scallions, tomato, pepper, nutmeg and salt.

Simmer one or two minutes. Add the ravioli and heat, tossing gently, for one minute more.

Serve hot with additional parmesan cheese. Yields four servings

# Chicken Crescent Roll Casserole
## Leila Sheriff

## Ingredients

2 or 3 Chicken breasts, cooked and chopped
2 8-Ounce Pillsbury crescent rolls
1 Can (10 ¾ ounces) cream of chicken soup
¾ Cup shredded cheddar cheese
½ Cup heavy cream
½ Chopped onion
4 Ounces softened cream cheese
4 Tablespoons of softened butter
4 Tablespoons mayo (more may be added)

## Directions

Mix heavy cream, half of the grated, shredded cheese, and chicken soup together and heat to melt cheese. Do not boil, put aside.

Mix cream cheese, butter, chicken, onion and mayo to smooth consistency.

Add garlic powder and pepper if you like.

(continued next page)

Spray Pyrex dish with Pam, pour 1/3 of mixture on bottom.

Unroll crescent rolls and fill with Cream Cheese mixture,

Roll up and lay them in Pyrex.

Pour the rest of the Heavy Cream mixture on top of the filled crescents and sprinkle with the remaining shredded cheese.

Bake 350° for 30-40 minutes till browned.

# Tamale Pie
## Linda Williams

My family grew up with this recipe as our Mother would make it often. I love this casserole as it brings back warm memories.

## Ingredients

1½ Pounds ground beef
Taco seasoning
1 Chopped onion
1 Can slice black olives
1 Can stewed tomatoes
1 Can black beans, drained and rinsed
½ Cup grated sharp cheddar cheese
1 Box cornbread mix
1 or 2 Cans green chili
1½ Cups grated sharp cheddar cheese

## Directions

Brown ground beef, taco seasoning and onion.
Meanwhile mix olives, tomatoes, black beans, and cheese.

(Continued next page)

Make cornbread mix as directed adding chilies and cheese to mixture.

In a 9 X 13 pan bottom layer is ground beef mixture.

Second layer is the tomato/bean mixture. Top layer is the cornbread mixture.

Bake at 350° for 30 – 40 minutes.

Serve with sour cream and salsa.

Good side dishes are Mexican rice and a salad.

# Spinach Quiche
## Betty Fontana

## Ingredients

1 Ready-made pie crust (I use Pillsbury)
3 Tablespoons butter
1 Small chopped onion
1 Cup frozen, chopped spinach, thawed and drained
1 Garlic clove (pressed, using garlic press)
4 Eggs
1 Cup milk
2 Cups shredded Colby-Monterey Jack cheese
Salt and pepper

## Directions

Preheat oven to 375.°
Press pie crust into 9" pie pan.
Pre-bake pie crust for about 10 minutes – set aside.
Sautee onion, garlic & spinach in butter until onion is soft – add salt & pepper and set aside.

(Continued next page)

In medium bowl whisk the eggs and milk. Spread shredded cheese in bottom of pie crust.

Spread spinach mixture over cheese in pie crust.

Pour egg/milk custard over spinach mixture and cheese.

Bake at 375° for 35 minutes. If crust starts to get too brown, cover edges with tinfoil.

Slice and serve.

# Ham and Egg Casserole
## Vivian Shay

## Ingredients

8-Ounce package of diced ham
9 Eggs, slightly beaten
3 Cups milk
1½ Teaspoon dry mustard
1 Teaspoon salt
5 Slices of white bread, torn into 1-inch pieces
1½ Cups grated cheddar cheese

## Directions

Mix eggs, milk, mustard and save.
Stir in bread, ham and cheese.
Pour into greased 13x9 inch casserole.
Refrigerate covered overnight.
Bake uncovered at 350° for 1 hour.

You may substitute 1 pound of browned, crumbled and drained sausage.

# Meatloaf
## Martha Chambers

## Ingredients

1½ Pounds ground beef
1/3 Cup finely chopped onions
3 Tablespoons Kikkoman soy sauce
¾ Cup dry breadcrumbs
½ Can condensed cream of mushroom soup
1 Egg
¼ Teaspoon pepper
¼ Teaspoon garlic powder

Sauce:
1½ Tablespoons Kikkoman soy sauce
1/3 Cup catsup
½ Can mushroom soup

## Directions

Combine ingredients for meat loaf. Mix
thoroughly. Pat to loaf shape and place in
roasting pan.
Combine sauce ingredients and mix well.
Pour over meat loaf.
Bake in 350° oven for 45 minutes.

# Wild Rice and Chicken
## Evelyn Fraley and Deane Dunnington

## Ingredients

1 6-Ounce Uncle Ben's Long Grain and
Wild Rice – Original
1/2 Cup butter
1/3 Cup chopped onions
1/3 Cup flour, salt & pepper
1 Cup canned milk or half & half
1 Cup chicken broth
2 Cups cubed chicken
1/3 Cup diced pimento
1/3 Cup chopped parsley
1/4 Cup slivered almonds

## Directions

Cook rice per package directions.
Melt butter. Add onions, flour, salt and
pepper. Stir in half and half and chicken
broth.
Cook until thick then stir in chicken and
other ingredients. Pour into greased baking
pan. Bake at 400° for 30 minutes
Makes 6 - 8 servings

# Spicy Shrimp Linguini
## Anonymous

## Ingredients

1 Pound of fresh shrimp
3 Julienned jalapeño peppers
3 Tablespoons olive oil
3 Tablespoons oyster sauce
Cilantro
3 Cloves garlic (minced)
3 Tablespoons Chinese black beans sauce
softened in hot water for 3½ minutes
1 Small box of linguine

## Directions

Cook linguine until al dente.
Sauté shrimp in a saucepan in 3 tablespoons
olive oil until done.
Add above ingredients except noodles. Add
oyster sauce then add cooked linguine. Stir
fry until coated.
Put in oven for 5 minutes at 400°.
Garnish with cilantro and serve with salad
and bread.

# Tuna-Noodle Casserole
## Mary Jane Raleigh

## Ingredients

3½ Cups medium noodles
2 7-Ounce cans tuna
½ Cup mayonnaise
1 Cup sliced celery
1/3 Cup chopped onions
1 Teaspoon salt
1 Can cream of mushroom soup
½ Cup milk
1 Cup shredded cheddar cheese
1 Can fried onion rings

## Directions

Cook noodles in boiling salted water until tender – drain.
Combine noodles, drained tuna, mayonnaise, celery and salt.
Blend in milk and soup, heat thoroughly.
Add cheese, heat and stir till cheese melts
Add noodle mixture.
Turn into ½ quart casserole.
Bake in a 425° oven about 25 minutes.

(Continued next page)

After first 5 minutes spread onion rings on top and continue baking 20 minutes more.

# Veggie Pizza
## Marlene Wells

## Ingredients

2 Large packages crescent rolls
1 16-Ounce package cream cheese softened
1 Envelope Knox vegetable soup
1 Cup mayo
1 Cup each green pepper, carrots,
cauliflower and white grated cheese
chopped fine

## Directions

Unwrap rolls onto large cookie sheet
pushing seams together to form crust.
Bake at 350.° Cool.
Mix cream cheese, soup mix and mayo.
Spread over crust.
Sprinkle on veggies.
Cover with wax paper and gently press
down into cream cheese mixture.
Sprinkle cheese on top and cut into small
squares using pizza cutter.
Can make a day ahead and cut a day ahead.
Yellow and red peppers may be used.

# Skillet Pork Chops
## Daisy Serle

## Ingredients

4 Pork loin or rib chops, (1-inch thick – about 1½ pounds)
¼ Cup beef flavored broth or chicken broth
4 Medium potatoes – cut into fourths
4 Small carrots cut into 1-inch pieces
4 Medium onions – cut into fourths
¾ Teaspoon salt
¼ Teaspoon pepper
Chopped fresh parsley, if desired

## Directions

Remove fat from pork. Spray 12-inch nonstick skillet with cooking spray; heat over medium-high heat.
Cook pork in skillet about 5 minutes, turning once, until brown. Add broth, potatoes, carrots and onions to skillet. Sprinkle with salt and pepper.
Heat to boiling; reduce heat.
Cover and simmer about 30 minutes or until vegetables are tender and pork is slightly pink when cut near bone.
Sprinkle with parsley.

# Ham Quiche
## Vivian Shay

## Ingredients

Pastry for 9-inch pie
1½ Cups shredded swiss cheese
1 Tablespoon all-purpose flour
½ Cup diced ham
4 Eggs, beaten
2 Cups half and half
½ Teaspoon dry mustard
¾ Teaspoon salt

## Directions

Prick bottom and sides of pastry with fork.

Bake at 400° for 3 minutes, remove from oven and gently prick with a fork.

Bake an additional 5 minutes.

Combine eggs, half and half, dry mustard and salt stirring well.

(Continued next page)

Pour mixture into pastry shell.
Bake at 325° for about 60 minutes or until set.

Let stand 10 minutes before serving.
Yield one nine-inch quiche.

You can create a variety of quiches by a simple substitute of main ingredients. Be bold and innovative. Enjoy!

## Summer Sausage Quiche

Substitute ½ diced summer sausage for ham.

## Mushroom Quiche

Sauté ½ pound sliced mushrooms and 1 small onion, chopped in 2 tablespoons vegetable oil; drain.
Substitute mushrooms and onion for ham and bake an additional 5 to 10 minutes.

# Broccoli Quiche
## Ann Hartnett

## Ingredients

1 14.1-Ounce package refrigerated pie crusts
6 Slices bacon
1½ Cups small broccoli florets
6 Large eggs
¾ Cups milk
⅔ Cup heavy whipping cream
½ Teaspoon salt
½ Teaspoon pepper
¾ Cup sharp shredded cheddar cheese, divided

## Directions

Preheat oven to 375.°
Unroll pie crusts and stack together on a clean work surface.  Roll crusts into a 14-inch circle.
Fit pie dough into a 9½ inch glass pie plate.
Fold over edges and crimp.
Using a fork prick bottom and sides of crust.

(Continued next page)

Line with parchment paper and fill with pie weights or dried beans.
Bake for 20 minutes or until lightly browned.
Remove weights and paper.
In a medium skillet cook bacon over medium heat until crisp.

Remove bacon to paper towels to drain.
Crumble bacon.
In a large saucepan cook broccoli florets in boiling salted water to cover for 3 to 4 minutes or until crisp-tender, drain.
Plunge into ice water to stop the cooking process, drain well and pat dry with paper towels.

In a large bowl whisk together eggs, milk, cream, salt and pepper until smooth and light in color.
Sprinkle bacon, broccoli and ½ cup cheese in baked crust.

Pour egg mixture over bacon mixture.
Bake for 20 minutes.  Sprinkle with remaining ¼ cheese and bake 10 minutes longer or until center is set.

# Spinach and Chicken Alfredo
## Daisy Serle

## Ingredients

4-6 Boneless, skinless chicken breasts
1 16-Ounce package of cooked spaghetti
2 Cups frozen spinach (thawed and drained)
1 14.5-Ounce can of seasoned diced
tomatoes (with basil and oregano)
3 Cloves garlic – minced
½ Yellow onion – chopped
¾ Cup milk
2/3 Cup parmesan cheese – grated
½ Cup heavy cream
½ Cup low-sodium chicken stock
2 Tablespoons cornstarch
½ Teaspoon dried basil
1 Teaspoon dried oregano
Olive oil, as needed
Kosher salt and freshly ground pepper, to
taste

## Directions

Heat olive oil in a large skillet over medium high
heat and brown chicken on all sides.

(Continued next page)

Continue cooking until chicken is cooked through and juices run clear.

Remove chicken from pan, cover with aluminum foil, and set aside.

Heat 2 tablespoons olive oil in the same skillet over medium-high heat and sauté onions for 6-8 minutes, or until softened and translucent.

Add garlic and cook for another 1 minute, or until fragrant.

Stir in tomatoes (with juices), chicken stock and spinach, and season with basil, oregano, salt and pepper.

In a small bowl, whisk cornstarch and milk to create a slurry, stirring until smooth. Pour slurry and heavy cream into sauce mixture. Bring to a gentle boil.

Stir in cheese until smooth and return chicken to pan. Cook for 5-10 minutes, or until chicken is warmed through. Pour over cooked spaghetti.

Serve hot and enjoy!

# Lasagna
## Daisy Serle

## Ingredients

1½ 6-Ounce boxes lasagna noodles
1 Cup finely chopped onions
1 Pound ground beef
Olive oil
1 Pound bulk Italian sausage (I use mild)
4 Cloves garlic – diced
Pinch crushed red pepper flakes
2 Cups ricotta
2 Cups grated Parmigiano-Reggiano, divided
2 Eggs
6 or 7 Basil leaves cut into small pieces
All-Purpose Marinara Sauce (I buy Barrilla marinara in jar) 2 jars usually makes one 9x13 pan of lasagna
1 Pound grated mozzarella
Salt and pepper

## Directions

Bring a large pot of well-salted water to a boil. Working batches, cook the lasagna

(Continued next page)

noodles until they are soft and pliable – not limp, 6 to 7 minutes.

Remove the pasta from the boiling water and lay flat on a sheet tray to cool. Reserve. Coat a large sauté pan with olive oil and bring to medium-high heat.
Add the sausage and ground beef and cook until brown and crumbly.

Remove from pan and reserve on paper towels.
Use same pan and sauté the garlic and onions and add to cooked sausage and beef.
In a small bowl, combine the ricotta, ½ the Parmigiano-Reggiano, the eggs, and the basil. Mix to combine well and season with salt and pepper.

Preheat the oven to 350.°

In the bottom of a 9 by 13-inch deep-dish baking dish, add a couple ladles of sauce and spread out in an even layer.
Arrange a layer of the lasagna noodles to completely cover the sauce.
Spread 1/3 of the ricotta mixture over the pasta and 1/3 of the meat.

Place a layer of pasta going in the other direction as the first layer. (this will give a little more stability)

Spread a light layer of sauce on the pasta and sprinkle 1/3 of the ricotta mixture and meat over the sauce.

Sprinkle a layer of mozzarella and some of the remaining Parmigiano-Reggiano over the pasta.

Repeat until all the ingredients have been used up or the pan is full. Be sure that there is a layer of pasta on top covered with sauce and sprinkled with mozzarella and Parmigiano.
Cover with foil.

Place the lasagna on a baking sheet and bake in the oven until the lasagna is hot and bubbly, about 1 hour 15 minutes, removing the foil for the last 15 minutes of cooking. Let cool for 20 minutes before slicing.

Note: For optimal slicing, make and bake the lasagna the day before. Heat it up again before slicing.

# Sausage Soufflé
## Pat Bankhead

## Ingredients

6 Slices bread
1 Pound pork sausage
1 Cup grated cheese
4 Eggs
1 Teaspoon salt
½ Teaspoon dry mustard
2 Cup milk

## Directions

Remove crusts from bread and cut into cubes.

Brown sausage.

Using an 8x8 casserole dish arrange layers of bread cubes and cover with cheese and sausage.

Repeat making 2 layers.
Mix remaining ingredients together and beat until smooth.

Pour over
casserole and
refrigerate
overnight.

Place in a pan
of water (I
don't do this)
and bake 45-60
minutes at
350.º

Great served
with roasted
potatoes, fruit and muffins.

(When I doubled this recipe, I used a 9 X 13
Pyrex and cooked it for about 1 hour and 20
minutes.)

# Chili for A Crowd
## Pat Bankhead

## Ingredients

4 Medium onions
2 Pounds ground beef
2 Cans (28 ounces each) diced tomatoes, not drained
1 Can (8 ounce) tomato sauce
1½ Tablespoons chili powder
1 Tablespoon sugar
2 Teaspoons salt
2 Cans (15-16 ounces each) kidney beans not drained

## Directions

Peel and chop the onions.

Cook the onions and beef in the Dutch oven over medium heat about 15 minutes, stirring occasionally, until beef is brown.

Place a large strainer over a medium bowl or place colander in a large bowl.

Spoon beef mixture into strainer to drain the fat. Discard fat. Return the beef mixture to the Dutch oven.

Stir in the tomatoes with their liquid, tomato sauce, chili powder, sugar and salt.
Heat to boiling over high heat.

Once mixture is boiling, reduce heat just enough so mixture bubbles gently. Cook uncovered 1 hour 15 minutes.

Stir the beans with their liquid into the chili. Heat to boiling over high heat. Once chili is boiling, reduce heat just enough so chili bubbles gently.

Cook uncovered about 15 minutes longer, stirring occasionally, until chili is thickened. Serves 12.

# Spaghetti Pie
## Rosemarie Galloway

## Ingredients

8 Ounces spaghetti (1/2 normal-sized box)
2 Tablespoon. butter
1/3 Cup grated parmesan cheese
2 Well beaten eggs
1 Pound ground beef
½ Cup chopped onions
1 Tablespoon dried Italian seasoning
¼ Cup chopped green peppers
8-Ounce can diced tomatoes
1 Cup cottage cheese
6-Ounce can tomato paste
1 Cup shredded mozzarella cheese (divided)

## Directions

Cook spaghetti according to package directions. Drain. Stir butter into hot spaghetti.

Stir in parmesan cheese and eggs.

Form spaghetti mixture into a crust in a 10-inch pie plate.

In a skillet cook ground beef, onion and green pepper until beef is browned. Drain off excess fat.

Stir in undrained tomatoes, tomato paste, and Italian seasoning. Heat mixture thoroughly.

Spread cottage cheese and ½ mozzarella cheese over bottom of spaghetti crust.

Fill pie with tomato/meat mixture. Bake uncovered in a preheated 350° oven for 25 minutes.

Remove from oven and sprinkle remaining mozzarella cheese on top. Bake 10 minutes longer until cheese melts.

Let stand for 5 minutes. Cut into wedges.

# Chicken Tetrazzini with Prosciutto and Peas
## Linda Williams

There are many variations to this popular dish, but this is definitely my favorite. Serves six.

## Ingredients

1 7-Ounce package vermicelli
3 Cups chopped cooked chicken
1 Cup (4 ounces shredded Parmesan cheese – reserve ½ cup)
1 Can cream of mushroom soup
1 10-Ounce container refrigerated Alfredo sauce
1 4-Ounce can sliced mushrooms, drained
3 Ounces finely chopped Prosciutto
1 Cup of frozen baby English peas – thawed
½ Cup chicken broth
¼ Cup dry white wine
¼ Teaspoon ground pepper
½ Cup slivered almonds

# Directions

Preheat over to 350.°

Prepare pasta according to package directions.

Sauté 3 ounces finely chopped prosciutto in 2 teaspoons of hot vegetable oil – in a small skillet over medium-high heat – 2 to 3 minutes or until crisp.

Stir together chicken, 1/2 cup Parmesan cheese, and next 8 ingredients, stir in pasta.

Spoon mixture into a lightly greased 11 x 7-inch baking dish.

Sprinkle with almonds and remaining 1/2 cup Parmesan cheese.

Bake at 350° for 35 minutes or until bubbly.

# Bistro Burgundy Stew
## Marilyn Barnini

## Ingredients

1 Pound boneless beef sirloin cut into 1½ inch pieces
3 Tablespoons all-purpose flour
6 Slices bacon cut into 1-inch pieces
2 Cloves garlic – crushed
3 Carrots – peeled and cut into 1-inch pieces (about 1½ cups)
¾ Cup Burgundy or other dry red wine
½ Cup Grey Poupon Dijon mustard
½ cup beef broth or lower sodium beef broth
12 small mushrooms
1½ Cups green onions, cut into 1 ½ inch pieces
Tomato rose and parsley for garnish
Breadsticks, optional

## Directions

Coat beef with flour, shaking off excess; set aside.

In large skillet over medium heat cook
bacon, just until done – pour off excess fat.
Add garlic – cook until browned.

Add carrots, wine, mustard and beef broth.

Heat to a boil – reduce heat.

Cover and simmer 30 minutes or until
carrots are tender, stirring occasionally.

Stir in mushrooms and green onions; cook
10 minutes more, stirring occasionally.

Garnish with tomato rose and parsley.

Serve with breadsticks, if desired.
Makes 4 servings.

# Pork Carnitas For Tacos
## Daisy Serle

## Ingredients

4 Pounds boneless pork butt, or shoulder,
cut into six equal pieces
2 Teaspoons salt
1 Teaspoon pepper
1 Tablespoon dried oregano
1 Tablespoon cumin
8 Cloves garlic – crushed
1 Medium onion – quartered
3 Leaves bay leaf
1 Lime – juiced
1 Large orange, juiced, save the spent halves

OPTIONAL TOPPINGS
Tortilla, taco shell
Rice
1 Can black beans
Salsa
Guacamole
Sour cream
Fresh cilantro
1 Cup cheese

## Directions

Cut pork into 6 equal pieces. Add it to the slow cooker.

Add salt, pepper, oregano, cumin, garlic, onion, bay leaves, lime juice and juice of the orange.
Add orange to the cooker as well. Mix together until the meat is well-coated.

Cover and cook on low for 8-10 hours, or until the meat pulls apart easily.

Remove the pork and transfer to a foil-lined baking sheet. Shred the pork and spread across the baking sheet in a single layer.

Pour about 1 cup of the liquid remaining in the slow cooker over the shredded pork.

Broil for 5-10 minutes until the meat browns and crisps along the edges.

Serve immediately.

Great as a filling in tacos, burritos, salads, or nachos!
Enjoy!

# Another Chicken and Broccoli Casserole
## Linda Williams

I named this *Another Chicken and Broccoli Casserole* as there are many recipes with similar ingredients. This has a nice flavor due to a dash of curry powder. A friend served it for dinner many years ago and graciously shared the recipe.

## Ingredients

2 Whole chicken breasts, skinned, cooked and boned
2 10-Ounce packages frozen broccoli
1 Can cream of chicken soup
½ Cup mayonnaise
½ Teaspoon.curry powder
1 Teaspoon lemon juice
1 Cup shredded cheddar cheese.
½ Cup buttered Pepperidge Farm breadcrumbs

## Directions

Place broccoli on bottom of baking dish.
Place cooked chicken over broccoli.

Mix together chicken soup, mayonnaise, lemon juice and curry powder and some of the cheese. Pour over chicken and broccoli.

Sprinkle remaining cheese over top (optional).

Sprinkle buttered breadcrumbs on top and bake at 350° for 25-30 minutes.

# Porcher House Company Chicken and Broccoli
## Linda Williams

Secretaries who worked at City Hall in Cocoa Village always knew what to expect on Secretary's Day. This was served at the Historical Porcher House every year but was always so welcomed. I have used this recipe many times for special occasions.

## Ingredients

3 to 4 Cups chicken – cooked and cut up
1 Can cream of chicken soup
¾ Cup mayonnaise
1 Bag cooked broccoli cuts
1 Cup Parmesan cheese
½ Box Jiffy Corn Muffin Mix
Sliced almonds to taste
1 Stick butter

## Directions

Mix chicken and broccoli cuts – spread in a 9 x 12 casserole.

Mix the mayonnaise and the soup and stir into the chicken and broccoli.

Combine the Parmesan cheese and corn muffin mix and sprinkle over the top.

Drizzle melted butter over everything, top with almonds and bake at 350º for about 25 minutes.

Note: The original recipe calls for 2 cans of cream of chicken soup and 1 cup of mayonnaise, so you can adjust it to your liking.

This dish may be frozen and better if made a day ahead.

Add the topping (Parmesan and corn muffin mix with butter and almonds) just before baking.

# SIDE DISHES

# SIDE DISHES
# TABLE OF CONTENTS

# Mixed Fruit Compote
## Rosemarie Galloway

## Ingredients

1 Cup golden raisins
1 Cup dried prunes
1 Cup dried apricots
2 Apples peeled and cut in small pieces
1 Can of sliced peaches (15 oz) with syrup
2 Cups of water
1 Cup of orange juice
2 Tablespoons honey
Zest and juice of one lemon
1 Teaspoon cinnamon
½ Teaspoon ground cloves

## Directions

In a medium heavy saucepan – combine all ingredients. Stir and bring to a slow boil. Reduce to simmer and cook until fruit is softened, and the liquid thickens.15-20 minutes.

Delicious with pork, ham, waffles or biscuits. For a little more kick, you can add ¼ cup brandy or orange liqueur.

# Carrot Soufflé
## Evelyn Fraley

## Ingredients

3 Cans of carrots, drained or 3 pounds fresh cooked
½ Cup butter
6 Large eggs
½ Cup all-purpose flour
Tablespoon baking powder
1½ Cups sugar
¼ Teaspoon ground cinnamon

## Directions

Process carrots and remaining ingredients in a food processor until smooth, stopping once to scrape down sides.
Spoon into 2 lightly greased 1½ quart soufflé baking dishes

Bake at 350° for 1 hour or until set and lightly browned.
Serve immediately.

Yields 16 servings (I usually make 2/3 of this recipe and it serves 12)

# Sweet Potatoes
## Bobbie Herlong

## Ingredients

Canned sweet potatoes
Brown sugar
Butter
Salt
Dash of nutmeg
Mini Marshmallows

## Directions

Beat canned potatoes in mix master.
Add brown sugar, butter, salt and dash of
nutmeg.

Cover top with tiny marshmallows.
Cook in buttered casserole at 350.º

# Vegetable Casserole
## Carol Beebe

## Ingredients

1 15-Ounce can shoepeg corn, drained
1 15-Ounce can sm. English peas, drained
1 15-Ounce can French cut green beans, drained
1 Cup sour cream
½ Cup chopped onion
1 Cup grated cheese
1 Cup cream of celery soup
1 Section Ritz crackers
½ Stick butter, melted
Slivered almonds (optional)

## Directions

Combine all ingredients except crackers and butter.
Stir gently so as not to break the vegetables.
Pour into greased casserole dish.
Combine Ritz crackers which have been crumbled with melted butter.
Sprinkle on top of vegetables and bake at 350° until bubbly all over.
Elegant side dish for a special dinner.

# Corn Pudding
## Daisy Serle

I got this recipe from my friend Fran Huntress who was one of the club's founders.

## Ingredients

½ Cup butter, softened
½ Cup sugar
2 Large eggs, room temperature
1 Cup sour cream
1 Package (8-1/2 ounces) Jiffy Mix
   cornbread
½ Cup 2% milk
1 15¼ Ounce can whole kernel corn, drained
1 14¾ Ounce can cream-style corn

## Directions

Preheat oven to 325°. In a large bowl, cream butter and sugar until light and fluffy.
Add eggs, one at a time, beating well after each addition.
Beat in sour cream.
Gradually add muffin mix alternately with milk. Fold in corn.

(Continued next page)

Pour into a greased 3-quart baking dish or 9x13 inch baking pan.

Bake, uncovered, until set and lightly browned, 45-50 minute

# Old Settlers Beans
## Pat Bankhead

## Ingredients

½ Pound fried bacon (or ½ pound cooked
hamburger or ½ pound cooked sausage)
½ Cup onions
1Small can lima beans drained well
1 Can kidney beans
1 Large can pork and beans
Salt and pepper
½ Cup catsup
1 Tablespoon mustard
½ Cup brown sugar
½ Cup barbecue sauce

## Directions

Mix everything together EXCEPT meat and
let stand overnight.
Next day add meat and bake for 1 hour at
325.º

# Green Beans and Friends
## Pat Bankhead

## Ingredients

1¼ Pounds fresh green beans, trimmed
Salt to taste
4 Slices bacon
2 Shallots – minced
1 Cup sliced mushrooms
¼ Teaspoon salt
1/8 Teaspoon pepper

## Directions

Blanch the green beans in salted boiling water for 5 minutes. Plunge into ice water to stop cooking and drain.
Sauté the bacon in a skillet until crisp.
Remove the bacon from the skillet, reserving the drippings.
Drain the bacon and chop into small pieces.
Sauté the shallots in the bacon drippings until soft.
Add the mushrooms and sauté until tender.
Add the drained green beans and cook until done to taste.
Season with ¼ teaspoon salt and pepper.

# Hot Apple Cider
## Monica Fischer

## Ingredients

2 quarts apple cider
2 cups orange juice
1 cup lemon juice
2 cups pineapple juice
2 sticks of cinnamon
1 teaspoon ground cloves

## Directions

Mix above, simmer, and serve warm.

I usually simmer in a large pot so the whole house smells like cinnamon apples!

# Kimmy's Macaroni and Cheese
## Daisy Serle

My daughter Kim makes this side dish every time her friends get together for a pool party. It's everybody's favorite.

## Ingredients

2 Sticks of butter
2 Cans evaporated milk
Small onion diced
16-Ounces Velveeta cheese
I Box Barilla Campanelle Pasta
Salt and pepper to taste

## Directions

Sauté a small onion, cut very small, in one stick of butter, until soft, on low heat, while the pasta cooks.

Add second stick of butter to onion mixture, two cans of evaporated milk and cheese cut into cubes.

Let the cheese mixture melt and get hot on low heat then add the cooked pasta to the mixture.

Pour out into a greased casserole dish and bake at 350° about 20 to 30 minutes with foil on top.

Take foil off stir and bake a few more minutes.

Remove from oven and top with cheddar or Monterey Jack if desired.

# SALADS

# SALADS TABLE OF CONTENTS

# Hollandaise Sauce
## Bobbie Herlong

## Ingredients

½ Stick butter
Juice of large lemon
1 Egg
Salt and pepper to taste

## Directions

Melt butter and let cool.

Beat egg and add to butter.

Gradually add lemon juice (stirring continually with wire whisk), salt and pepper.

Simmer until right consistency, always stirring with wire whisk.

# Pasta Salad
## Bobbie Herlong

## Ingredients (Mostly optional)

1 Pound package of pasta
Italian Dressing
Chopped scallions
Cooked Broccoli
Sliced Tomatoes
Cheese
Celery and Green Peppers
Mushrooms
Artichoke hearts
Radishes
Lawry's seasoned Salt
Lemon Pepper

## Directions

Cool a 16-ounce package of your choice of
pasta. Drain.
Add your choice of Italian dressing,
chopped scallions.  Marinate overnight.
Add broccoli, sliced tomatoes, cheese,
celery, green peppers, mushrooms, artichoke
hearts, radishes. Add Lawry seasoned salt
and lemon pepper to taste.

# Best Sawmill Gravy Ever
## Bill Serle

In the throes of putting this cookbook together, I received the following from an old friend: "I just made the best sawmill gravy that I ever tasted. I love sawmill gravy in the summer with sliced tomatoes and in the winter over a baked sweet potato. And, of course, I love it in the mornings with scrambled eggs and biscuits. The best thing about my gravy is that **I don't allow any dead pigs in my gravy.**"

## Ingredients

2 Morning Star Vegetarian Sausage patties
Olive oil to cover bottom of 10-inch skillet
6 Heaping Tablespoons of whole wheat flour
Sage, black pepper, and smoked paprika to taste – be generous
About a quart of milk

(Continued next page)

## Directions

Start by cooking two Morning Star vegetarian sausage patties – chopped.

Cover the bottom of a ten-inch skillet with olive oil and put it over medium heat. When the olive oil is hot, stir in 6 heaping tablespoons of plain whole wheat flour.

At this point, add more olive oil if needed to make a good rue.

While stirring to brown the flour, add a generous amount of sage, black pepper, and smoked paprika.

Add the cooked, chopped sausage.

When the rue is nice and brown, stir in almost a quart of milk and stir continuously until it comes to a good rolling boil. (It has to come to a boil before it will thicken)

"Dump the gravy into an old Fire King gravy bowl that has a handle and spout. There is something about an old bowl that makes the gravy better."

# Cranberry Gelatin Salad
## Evelyn Fraley

## Ingredients

2 3-Ounce package raspberry gelatin
16-Ounce can whole berry, cranberry Sauce
20-Ounce can crushed pineapple (undrained)
½ Package unflavored gelatin*
2 Cups boiling water
½ to 1 Cup broken pecans
½ Cup chopped celery (optional for crunch)

## Directions

Mix gelatins together add boiling water.

Add cranberry sauce and stir until dissolved.

Add pineapple with juice, pecans and celery.

Pour in mold and refrigerate.

Serves 12

*I don't use the unflavored gelatin but used
a little less boiling water.

# Homemade Caesar Salad Dressing
## Pat Bankhead

## Ingredients

2 Small garlic cloves – minced
1 Teaspoon anchovy paste (usually found near the tuna fish in supermarkets)
2 Tablespoons freshly squeezed lemon juice,
1 Teaspoon Dijon mustard
1 Teaspoon Worcestershire sauce
1 Cup mayonnaise, best quality such as Hellmann's Real
½ Cup freshly grated Parmigiano-Reggiano (I have used other brands)
¼ Teaspoon salt
¼ Teaspoon freshly ground black pepper

## Instructions:

In a medium bowl, whisk together the garlic, anchovy paste, lemon juice, Dijon mustard and Worcestershire sauce.

Add mayonnaise, Parmesan, salt and pepper, and whisk until well combined.

# Crunchy Pea and Cauliflower Salad
## Evelyn Fraley

## Ingredients

1 10-Ounce package frozen baby peas, thawed
1 Cup diced celery
1 Cup chopped cauliflower
¼ cup diced green onion (I left this out)
1 Cup chopped cashews
½ Cup sour cream
1 Cup prepared Hidden Valley Ranch original salad dressing

## Directions

Mix and serve.

Crisp, cooked, crumbled bacon for garnish (optional)

# Hot Chicken Salad
## Marilyn Barnini

## Ingredients

4 – 6 Cups cooked diced chicken
2 Cups diced celery
4 Hard boiled eggs
2 Cups cream chicken soup
1 Cup mayonnaise
4 Teaspoon grated onion
2 Teaspoon lemon juice
Dash of Worcestershire sauce
1 Large can of mushrooms
¼ Cup slivered almonds
¼ Cup breadcrumbs

## Directions

Combine all of above ingredients except crumbs and slivered almonds.

Mix well. Put in casserole dish.

Top with crumbs and almonds.

Bake at 400° for 25-30 minutes.

# Chicken Chutney Salad
## Linda Williams

## Ingredients

2 Cups of chicken – breast meat, cooked and diced
1 8-Ounce can pineapple tidbits, drained
1 Cup diced celery
½ Cup green onion, sliced
½ Cup salted peanuts
2/3 Cup mayonnaise
2 Tablespoons chopped chutney,
½ Teaspoon lime rind, grated
½ Teaspoon curry powder
¼ Teaspoon salt
Black pepper to taste
Garlic salt to taste
Lettuce greens

## Directions

Mix first ingredients and toss with lettuce to make a salad.

# Creamy Jell-O Salad
## Lyn Davidson

## Ingredients

1 Large raspberry Jell-O package
1 Can cranberry sauce (I use whole berry)
½ Cup burgundy wine
1 Small can of crushed pineapple (drained)
1 8-Ounce cream cheese (soft)
2 Teaspoons sugar
1 Carton cool whip
Pecans or walnuts (small pieces)

## Directions

Mix Jell-O, cranberry sauce with 2 cups boiling water.
Add burgundy and pineapple and some nuts.
Put in 11x8 dish (or any favorite dish) and chill overnight.

Next day....
Mix soft cream cheese with sugar
Fold into cool whip and spread over Jell-O
Add chopped nuts

# Macaroni Salad
## Daisy Serle

This recipe comes from my BFF Gail Mangione. She gave it to me when I owned a restaurant in Miami. Our customers loved it.

## Ingredients

1 16-Ounce package elbow macaroni
¼ Cup (or more) of Marzetti coleslaw salad dressing
Add Miracle Whip to taste
2 Tablespoons sweet pickles cubed
½ Large green bell pepper
1 Tiny jar pimento
2 or 3 Slices American cheese cut very small
2 or 3 Tablespoons grated onion
5 Hard-boiled eggs – chopped fine
Salt and pepper to taste.

## Directions

Cook and cool elbow macaroni.
Mix it all up and serve with a smile.

# Slaw Salad
## Mary Jane Raleigh

## Ingredients

2 Packages Ramen noodles (beef)
2 Packages of broccoli slaw
1 Cup canola oil
1 Cup sugar
½ Cup Tarragon wine vinegar
2 Cups sunflower seeds

## Directions

Mix liquid ingredients and sugar and packets
of Ramen Noodle beef flavoring.

Pour over slaw.

Just before serving, add crunched Ramen
noodles.

# White Bean Tomato Salad
## Monica Fischer

## Ingredients

2 cans white beans, canned, rinsed, and drained
3 Medium tomatoes – seeded and chopped
¼ Cup minced fresh parsley
1 Tablespoon fresh basil
2 Tablespoons balsamic vinegar
4 Tablespoons olive oil
1/8 Teaspoon ground pepper
1/8 Teaspoon salt
½ Medium red onion, diced

## Directions

Mix all together well. Adjust seasoning to your taste, refrigerate, and serve chilled.

# Copper Pennies
## Monica Fischer

## Ingredients

2 Pounds carrots
1 small red onion
1 bell pepper
½ Cup olive oil
¾ Cup red wine vinegar
1 Cup sugar
1 Teaspoon Worcestershire sauce
1 Teaspoon prepared mustard
1 Can of condensed tomato soup

## Directions

Clean, slice, and cook carrots until tender.

Dice red onion and bell pepper then add to carrots.

Mix remaining ingredients and pour over carrots. Chill overnight.

# Mardi Gras Salad
## Gail Holder

## Ingredients

2 Teaspoons finely chopped onion
½ cup cider vinegar
¼ Cup sugar
¼ Cup olive oil
1 Teaspoon ground dry mustard
4 Slices, crisply fried, crumbled bacon
1 10-Ounce package baby spinach
½ Cup chopped red onion
2 1-Ounce cans mandarin oranges, drained
1/3 Cup shredded carrots
1 Head red lettuce torn into pieces

## Directions

In small bowl, whisk together onion,
vinegar, sugar, olive oil and mustard.
Refrigerate until ready to toss the salad.
In large bowl combine lettuce, spinach, red
onion, mandarin oranges, carrots and bacon.
Toss salad with the dressing

Yield 8-10 servings.

# Pickled Peppers (Mini Peppers)
## Evelyn Fraley

## Ingredients

1 Small bag mini sweet peppers (12 – 15 mini peppers)
1 Small onion – sliced
¼ Cup extra virgin olive oil
½ Teaspoon kosher salt
3 Garlic cloves
1 Cup rice vinegar (or white vinegar)
1 cup stuffed green olives
2/3 Cup sour orange juice (or ½ cup orange juice and ¼ lime juice)
(I use ¼ cup honey and I do not use sour orange juice.)

## Directions

Place all ingredients in saucepan, except sour orange juice, on medium.
Simmer and stir 20-30 minutes or until peppers are fork tender.
Remove mixture from pan, stir in orange juice. Place mixture in refrigerator and chill overnight. Store in an airtight container until ready to serve.

# Greek Pasta Salad
## (for a large party)
### Evelyn Fraley

## Ingredients

2 1-Pound boxes Barilla Mezze Penne
(small penne pasta), cooked

(I added a small amount of salt, minced garlic, basil,
oregano and parsley to pasta when cooking so the
pasta has some flavor)

8 Ounces crumbled Feta cheese
Small jar of Mezzetta Kalamata pitted Greek
olives
6 Ounces fresh baby spinach
Ken's Greek dressing to taste

## Directions

Mix all and serve.

# Chicken Salad
## Daisy Serle

## Ingredients

2½ Cups cooked chicken chunks
½ Cup mayo
1/3 Cup sour cream
1 Cup grapes halved
1 Cup chopped walnuts
½ Cup Craisins
Salt and Pepper to taste
½ Cup celery chopped very fine
Dill weed to taste

## Directions

Mix and serve.

Sometimes I add a cup of frozen tiny peas (thawed)

# Jan's Tomatoes
## Daisy Serle

## Ingredients

Six large ripe tomatoes
¼ Cup Extra Virgin Olive Oil
1 Tablespoon Basil (or Tarragon)
Vinegar (or whatever vinegar you have)
1 Tablespoon Grey Poupon Mustard
1 Tablespoons FRESH Chopped Parsley (I usually do 3-4 Tablespoons)
1 Teaspoon Lawry's Garlic Salt
1 Teaspoon McCormick's Lemon Pepper
½ Teaspoon Dried Dill Weed
½ Teaspoon Dried Basil
½ Teaspoon Dried Tarragon

## Directions

Peel Tomatoes (Can do day ahead of serving and wrap tightly in sandwich baggies or plastic.)
Slice Tomatoes Thickly

DRESSING:
(Enough for about 6 tomatoes)

(Continued next page)

Whisk oil and vinegar and then SLOWLY whisk into the mustard. Can make this a day ahead.

You can measure dry ingredients day ahead. But best to add to oil/mustard late on "serving day" (along with parsley, below) because herbs tend to get "tired" after being put in liquid.

Thoroughly mix, shake or whisk dressing close to serving time. Arrange sliced tomatoes on platter and, using teaspoon or other small spoon, spread with dressing.

Note: I have used leftover dressing for a week or more after it has been mixed. It is still good, but just not quite as good as when freshly assembled.

# Ramen Noodle Salad
## Evelyn Fraley

## Ingredients

4 Cups shredded green cabbage
2 Cups shredded red cabbage
1 Cup shredded carrots
2 Packages ramen noodles – broken into chunks, seasoning packets reserved
½ Cup sliced green onions
½ Cup toasted slivered almonds
½ Cup vegetable oil
1/3 Cup rice vinegar
2 Tablespoons sugar

## Directions

Mix and Serve.

# Broccoli Salad
## Pat Bankhead

## Ingredients

SALAD:
2 Small heads broccoli
1 Pound sliced bacon
1 Sweet onion (I use a red onion.)
½ Cup seedless raisins (Craisins okay too)

## Directions

Separate broccoli flowers from stems and save stems for another use. Fry and crumble bacon. Slice or dice onion fine, add raisins and toss all together.

DRESSING:
1 Cup mayonnaise, 2 Tablespoons vinegar, ½ Cup sugar

## Directions

Mix well and pour dressing over broccoli mixture. Refrigerate two hours or longer. Serves 10 – 12. (I only use half of the dressing on this amount of salad.)

# Shrimp Pasta Salad
## Vivian Shay

## Ingredients

24 Ounces cooked popcorn shrimp
16 Ounces Shell pasta. (Medium)
1 Cup chopped celery
2 Teaspoons lemon juice
1/8 Teaspoons pepper
Salt to taste
½ Cup Miracle Whip mayonnaise
4 or 5 Sliced green onions

## Directions

Shell Shrimp
Cook, drain and cool Pasta
Add other ingredients and garnish with
lemon wedges.

Chill before serving.

# Balsamic Pear Salad
## Pat Bankhead

## Ingredients

Salad greens
1 or 2 Pears sliced – (I used Bosc and Red Pears)
¼ Cup dried cherries – (Craisins can be substituted)
Balsamic Dressing (See below)
Glazed pecans (See below)
Crumbled blue cheese - or any cheese

BALSAMIC DRESSING:
¼ Cup balsamic vinegar
¼ Cup extra virgin olive oil
1 Shallot minced
Pinch each sea salt and black pepper

## Directions

DRESSING DIRECTIONS
Mix well shaking or whisking. Can be doubled or tripled.

GLAZED PECANS:
2 Tablespoons brown sugar, firmly packed
2 Teaspoons butter
2 Teaspoons light corn syrup
1/8 Teaspoon salt
1 Cup pecan halves

PECAN DIRECTIONS:
Combine pecan ingredients in a large skillet.
Stir over medium heat until butter is melted.
Add pecans and cook, stirring constantly, for
5-7 minutes. (I cooked 5 minutes and they
were a little sticky. Maybe 7 minutes next
time.) Make sure pecans are all coated
evenly.
Spread pecans in single layer on parchment
paper and cool completely.
Separate.

## Serving Directions

To serve combine greens, half of the sliced
pear, dried cherries, and half of pecans.
Drizzle with dressing and toss to combine.
Plate and garnish with remaining pears and
pecans.
I also added crumbled blue cheese to the
top.

# Strawberry and Cream Salad
## Pat Bankhead

## Ingredients

2 3-Ounce packages strawberry jello
2 Cups boiling water
2 10-Ounce packages frozen strawberries
1 20-Ounce can crushed pineapple
3 Medium bananas mashed
½ Cup chopped pecans
1 8-Ounce container sour cream

## Directions

Dissolve gelatin in boiling water.
Stir in fruit and nuts.
Pour half the gelatin mixture into a 9X13 pan. (I use a trifle bowl and make 3 layers.) Chill until firm. Store remaining gelatin mixture at room temperature while making the remaining layers. Spoon sour cream over congealed fruit mixture.
Keep layering ending with sour cream on top.
Garnish with whole strawberries. Serves 12-18.

# Ham and Pasta Salad
## Vivian Shay

## Ingredients

I – 3 Cups uncooked small pasta
2 Cups frozen peas
3 Cups diced ham
1 Cup sliced celery
1 Cup chopped red bell pepper
½ cup dill pickle relish (drained)
8 Ounces Colby Monterey Jack cheese
(diced 2 cups)
¾ Cup chopped chives
1/8 Teaspoon pepper
¾ Cup mayonnaise


## Directions

Cook pasta as directed and, last 2 to 3
minutes, add peas. Rinse, drain and cool.
Mix ham, celery, bell pepper, relish and
cheese.
Mix all remaining solid ingredients.
Add mayo and toss to coat.
Serve or chill.

# Bok Choy Salad
## Linda Williams

Brown the following and then let cool:

## Ingredients

1 Stick butter
2 Packages crushed Ramen noodles
½ Cup sesame seeds or 1 Cup sunflower seeds
1 Small Package slivered almonds

Add to the cooled ingredients listed above:
1 Head bok choy, chopped
1 Bunch chopped scallions

## Dressing:

½ Cup Sugar
½ Cup Sesame oil
¼ Cup white vinegar
2 Tablespoons soy sauce

Mix all together and enjoy!

# Broccoli Salad
## Linda Williams

## Ingredients

2 Heads broccoli
½ Pound bacon
1 Cup honey-roasted peanuts
1 Cup raisins
1 Small red onion (Optional)

**Dressing:**

½ Cup sugar
1 Cup mayonnaise
2 Tablespoons cider vinegar

## Directions

Chop broccoli in small pieces – florets only.
Chop up bacon and fry until crisp.

Place all salad ingredients in a large bowl.
Mix together all dressing ingredients.
Pour over salad.
Marinate for a couple of hours.
Top with shredded mozzarella cheese, if
desired.

# Buttermilk Potato Salad
## Linda Williams

Note – Not everyone likes or can eat mayonnaise,
so this is a nice alternative.

## Ingredients

3 Pounds small red potatoes
¼ Cup plus 1 tablespoon crème fraiche or
sour cream
1/3 Cup low-fat buttermilk
2 Tablespoons prepared horseradish
2 Teaspoons coarse salt
¼ Teaspoon freshly ground pepper
¼ Cup dill sprigs
¼ Cup finely chopped fresh chives

## Directions

Cover potatoes with water by 1½ inches in a
2-quart pot and bring to a boil. Reduce heat,
and simmer until potatoes can be pierced
easily with the tip of a knife, about 20
minutes.
Drain and let cool completely.
Cut potatoes into halves, or quarter if large.

Stir potatoes, crème fraiche, buttermilk, horseradish, salt and pepper together in a bowl. Gently stir in herbs just before serving.

# Purple Salad
## Betty Adamson

## Ingredients

2 Packages Dream Whip, very cold and well whipped
1 Can Bing black Cherries, well drained and cut with scissors
1 8-Ounce package cream cheese – blended with ¼ Cup juice from cherries
1 Can crushed pineapple, drained
1 Cup small marshmallows

## Directions

Follow box directions for Dream Whip.
Mix all and serve.

# Vegetable Marinated Salad
## Marilyn Barnini

## Ingredients

1 Cup sugar
½ Cup oil
¾ Cup vinegar
1 Cup diced celery
8 Green onions small
1 Jar pimentos – chopped
1 Can Le Sueur peas – drained
1 Can water chestnuts, sliced
1 Can shoe peg corn
1 Green pepper – diced
1 Can French-style green beans, drained
Salt and pepper – to taste

## Directions

Make marinade from first 3 ingredients.
Add vegetables and mix.
Store overnight in refrigerator.
Will keep for 3 days.

# Japanese Chicken Salad
## Roz McClure

## Ingredients

2 Tablespoons salad oil
½ Cup sliced almonds
2 Tablespoons sesame seed
1 Package (3 oz) Ramen noodle soup mix
(crumble noodles inside package – flavor
packet not needed)
2 Cups cooked chicken, diced or shredded
4 Cups finely shredded green cabbage
½ Cup chopped green onions with tops
Salt
Dressing (recipe follows)

## Directions

Place oil in a 10- to 12-inch frying pan over
medium-high heat.
When oil is hot, add almonds, sesame seed,
and noodles – stir-fry until mixture is lightly
browned, 3 to 4 minutes.
Scoop mixture from pan with a slotted
spoon and drain on paper towels.

In a salad bowl, combine noodle mixture, chicken, cabbage, onions, and dressing; add salt to taste and mix well.

DRESSING: Stir together 1/3 cup each salad oil and rice vinegar or white distilled vinegar, 5 teaspoons sugar, and ½ teaspoon pepper

Makes 6 servings.

# DESSERTS

# DESSERTS TABLE OF CONTENTS

# Peanut Butter Pie
## Bobbie Herlong

## Ingredients

¼ Cup peanut butter
1 Cup Cool Whip
2 Cups vanilla ice cream
1 Small package instant vanilla pudding

## Directions

Mix and pour into graham cracker shell.
Freeze until solid.

# Cheesecake
## Daisy Serle

My friend Terry Discenza brought this cheesecake to a luncheon and it was delicious. The orange and lemon rind give it a great taste.

## Ingredients

CRUST
2¼ cup graham cracker crumbs
½ cup sugar
½ cup of butter

Combine ingredients and press into the bottom and 2/3 of the way up the side of a greased 10" spring-form pan. Can use cooking spray to grease pan.

CHEESECAKE
5 8-Ounce packages cream cheese
2 Cups of sugar
2 Tablespoons flour
1 Tablespoon fresh grated orange rind
1 Tablespoon fresh grated lemon rind
6 Eggs (at room temperature)
8 Ounces heavy cream

# Directions

Soften cream cheese in microwave then beat until smooth and creamy

Sift together sugar and flour and gradually beat into cream cheese.

Beat in orange and lemon rinds

Beat in eggs gradually keeping mixture smooth.

Fold in cream until blended
well and put into prepared crust.

Preheat oven to 400,° turn down to 200.°
Bake cheesecake for 3½ hours.
Baking times may vary according to your oven.

Non-stick springform pans take less time.
Let cool thoroughly then refrigerate.

Freezes well.

# Easy to Prepare Apple Cake.
## Carol Scott

## Ingredients

3 Eggs
1 Cup sugar
½ Cup shortening
1 1/3 Cup flour
1 Teaspoon baking powder
1½ Pounds apples
1/3 Cup sugar
Teaspoon cinnamon

## Directions

Cream shortening and sugar.

Add eggs and mix well.
Combine flour and baking powder and then
add to batter, mixing thoroughly.
Cut apples in slices. Sprinkle with sugar and
cinnamon.

Grease 8x8 pan. Put half the batter in pan,
add apples, and cover with rest of the batter.
Bake 1 hour in a preheated 350° oven.

# Necia's Ice Cream Sandwiches
## Leila Sheriff

## Ingredients

2 12-Packs ice cream sandwiches
1 Large cool whip
1 Package heath or toffee chips
Chocolate fudge syrup
Caramel fudge syrup

## Directions

Layer ice cream sandwiches. (10 or 12)
With ½ cool whip bucket.
Swirl with chocolate fudge.
Swirl with caramel.
Sprinkle with toffee chips
Repeat for another layer.

Freeze night before.

# Easy Pumpkin Layer Cheesecake
## Rosemarie Galloway

## Ingredients

2 8-Ounce packages of softened
Philadelphia cream cheese
½ Cup sugar
½ Teaspoon vanilla
2 Eggs
½ Cup canned pumpkin
Dash each of ground cloves and nutmeg
1 Ready-to-use graham cracker crumb crust

## Directions

Blend well, cream cheese, sugar and vanilla
with electric mixer on medium speed.
Add eggs and mix until blended.
Stir pumpkin and spices into 1 cup of the
batter.
Pour remaining plain batter into crust. Top
with pumpkin spice batter.
Bake at 350° for 35-40 minutes or until
center is almost set.
Cool. Refrigerate three hours or overnight.
Makes 8 servings.

# Sinfully Delicious Chocolate Cake
## Marilyn Barnini

## Ingredients

1 12-Ounce package semi-sweet chocolate chips (add these last)
1 Package chocolate cake mix-dark devil's food mix
1 Package instant chocolate pudding
1 Cup sour cream
4 Eggs
½ Cup oil
¼ Cup warm water
¼ Cup Amoretto or 1 teaspoon almond extract

## Directions

Mix above at least 3 minutes.
Add chips.
Bake in greased Bundt pan <u>dusted with cocoa, not flour</u>
Bake at 350º for 40-50 minutes.
Serve warm with ice cream.

# Chocolate "Pecan Pie" Truffles
## Rosemarie Galloway

## Ingredients

2½ Cups pecans, toasted and finely chopped
1 Cup graham cracker crumbs
1 Cup dark-brown sugar – packed
½ Teaspoon salt
2 Tablespoons maple syrup
¼ Cup bourbon
1 Teaspoon vanilla
7 Ounces dark chocolate

## Directions

In a medium bowl, stir together the pecans, graham cracker crumbs, brown sugar and salt until well combined.

Add the maple syrup, bourbon and vanilla, stirring thoroughly.

Use your hands to make sure the mixture becomes fully incorporated.

Form the mixture into walnut-sized balls, then place on a sheet pan and freeze for 2 hours.

In the top of a double boiler or a medium stainless-steel bowl over a pot of gently simmering water, melt chocolate.

Line a baking sheet with parchment paper. Dip the frozen balls into the melted chocolate, then place onto prepared baking sheet.

Let sit for 15 minutes or until firm. Truffles should be stored at room temperature in an airtight container.

Tip: I use a 12-ounce bag of semi-sweet chocolate chip and a little drizzle of oil for consistency and gloss. Delicious.

# Peppermint Melt-Away Cookies
## (makes 48)
## Marlene Wells

## Ingredients

Canola spray
1 8-ounce Package cream cheese
½ cup unsalted butter
1 Starlight mints (large zip-lock bag finely crushed) – divided
1 Large egg
½ Teaspoon vanilla
1 16.5-Ounce box Duncan Hines Classic White cake mix – divided
1 Cup Nestle's premier white toll house morsels

## Directions

Preheat oven to 350º.
Coat baking sheets with spray.
Cut cream cheese and butter into small pieces and place in large bowl to soften.
Crush mints in zip-lock bag – Add to cream cheese. (set aside ½ cup crushed mints)
Add egg, vanilla and one-half of cake mix.

Mix with electric mixer 1-2 minutes or until thoroughly blended.
Place remaining ½ cup mints in shallow bowl.

Shape dough into 1-inch balls and press tops of dough into mints.

Place in baking sheets, mint side up and two inches apart.

Bake 10-12 minutes.

Transfer to wire racks to cool.

# Strawberry Earthquake Cake
## Rosemarie Galloway

## Ingredients

1½ Cup of fresh Florida strawberries
1¼ Cups confectioner's sugar
1 Box white or yellow cake mix
1 to 1½ Cups shredded coconut
8 Ounces cream cheese

## Directions

Mix cake according to package instructions.
Grease and flour 9 by13 inch pan
Layer about 1 cup or more of coconut on
bottom of pan
Pour half of the mixed cake batter over the
coconut
Cream together the cream cheese,
confectioner sugar, and 1 cup of mashed,
fresh strawberries.  Drop cream cheese
mixture in large dollops over cake mix
Pour remaining half of cake mix over top.
Bake at 350° for 28-30 minutes.
Enjoy.

# Aunt Daisy's Old-Fashioned Sugar Cookies
## Monica Fischer

## Ingredients

4 to 5 Cups Flour (Enough to form dough)
2 Cups sugar / 1 white, 1 brown
1 Cup Crisco or oil
1 Cup sour milk (use milk with two tablespoons vinegar)
1 Egg
1 Teaspoon baking soda
Pinch of salt
1 Teaspoon of vanilla

## Directions

Mix sugar, Crisco, milk, egg, and vanilla
Combine baking soda salt with the flour and slowly add to wet ingredients,

Roll dough and cut into circles and sprinkle with sugar.

Bake at 375° until brown on edges.
These cookies will be very dry and thick – just perfect for dunking.

# Best Gingerbread I Have Ever Eaten
## Gail Holder

## Ingredients

1¼ Cups flour, plus extra for pan
1 Teaspoon cinnamon
1 Teaspoon cloves
¼ Cup butter, plus extra for pan
1 Teaspoon baking powder
1 Teaspoon ginger
½ Teaspoon salt
¼ Cup sugar
¾ Cup boiling water
¾ Teaspoon baking soda
1 Egg, lightly beaten
1/3 Cup molasses

## Directions

Sift together the flour, baking powder, cinnamon, ginger, cloves and salt
In a separate bowl, combine the butter and sugar until the mixture is well mixed.
Beat ½ teaspoon of the baking soda into the molasses and mix well. – add to butter and sugar.

Add the remaining ¼ teaspoon baking soda to ¾ cup boiling water and stir.

Alternately, with the sifted dry ingredients, add the water to the butter mixture

Fold in the beaten egg.

Pour into a greased and floured 8-inch square pan.

This mixture will seem too thin, but do not increase the quantity of flour as many doubting cooks have tried to do.

Bake in preheated 325° oven for 30 minutes or until a toothpick inserted in the middle comes out clean.

Eat as is or top with whipped cream, ice cream or wine sauce.

9 servings.

# Hummingbird Cake
## Betty Fontana

3 Cups flour
2 Cups sugar
2 Cups bananas (diced)
1 Cup cooking oil
8 Ounce can crushed pineapple (with juice)
1 Teaspoon salt
1 Teaspoon cinnamon
1 Teaspoon soda
1 Teaspoon vanilla
3 Eggs
1 Cup chopped pecans

## Directions

Mix dry ingredients
Add the rest and stir well
Do not beat.

Grease and flour 9" tube pan.

Pour ingredients into pan and bake at 350°
for 1 hour or until done.

(I use Pillsbury cream cheese frosting).

# Pineapple/Cheese Recipe
## Betty Fontana

## Ingredients

3 15-Ounce cans pineapple tidbits (or chunks cut smaller if tidbits not available), drained
1½ Cups white sugar
1 Cup all-purpose flour
3 Cups shredded cheddar cheese
3 to 4 Dozen Ritz crackers, crumbled
¾ Cup melted butter

## Directions

Preheat oven to 350.°
In a bowl, stir together the drained pineapple, sugar, flour, and cheese.
Spread in a 13x9 dish

Sprinkle crumbled crackers over the top. Pour melted butter over the top and bake for 30 minutes or until cheese is melted well.

That's it! Super easy.

# Apple Pan Dowdy
## Bill Serle

A favorite dessert from the time I was a kid. It is super easy to make and very forgiving.

## Ingredients

1 20-Ounce can Sliced Apples
1 Stick of cold butter
1/3 Cup water
1 1/3 Cup Sugar
1 Cup Flour
1 Teaspoon ground cinnamon
1 Tablespoon of lemon juice

## Directions

Spread the apples in a greased, round pan. Sprinkle the water, lemon juice and cinnamon on top. Stir a little if you wish. Mix sugar and flour in a bowl. Make a crumb topping by forking cold butter into the sugar and flour mix.

The forking technique is important. You can use a knife and fork together and create a crumb like mixture and NOT a creamy or dough-like mass. Use the edge of the fork.

This crumb factor provides a crunch that is so pleasing.
Sprinkle the crumb topping on the apples and bake 400° for 40 minutes.
Be patient.

Cool a little.

Keep ice cream handy in case you burn your tongue.

♪♪ Shoo Fly Fly and Apple Pan Dowdy makes my eyes light up and my stomach say, "Howdy." I never get enough of that wonderful stuff...♪♪

# Very Lemon Cream
## Bill Serle

I have enjoyed making and eating this astounding
recipe many times. To try it is to love it.

## Ingredients

1¾ Cups crushed Vanilla Wafers
1½ Cups sugar
9 Tablespoons Lemon Juice (3 good lemons)
3 Cups heavy cream
6 Separated eggs
½ Teaspoon of salt

Directions

Line the bottom of an ungreased 9-inch
spring form pan with one cup of crushed
vanilla wafers.
In a small bowl, stir the sugar into the lemon
juice.
Whip cream in a heavy bowl – reserve.
Beat yolks a little with salt in another bowl –
reserve.

Beat egg whites, in a clean bowl, until stiff, but not dry.

Fold egg yolks into the lemon juice and sugar mixture.

Fold whipped cream, lemon juice mixture and whipped egg whites in a large bowl and pour into the spring form pan on top of the crumbs. Don't over stir – little swirls of lemon are fine.

Top with remaining crumbs, cover and freeze hard.

Don't defrost. (It will be just right frozen – even after a few minutes on the plates.)

Unspring pan and slice with a big kitchen knife and serve.

It's beautiful, and it will serve sixteen.

# Bacardi Rum Cake
## Evelyn Fraley

## Ingredients

1 Cup chopped pecans or walnuts
1 Package yellow cake mix (I use lemon)
1 Package Jell-O instant vanilla pudding mix
4 Eggs
½ Cup cold water
½ Cup Wesson oil
½ Cup dark rum

GLAZE
¼ Pound butter
¼ Cup water
1 Cup granulated sugar
½ Cup dark rum

## Directions

Preheat oven to 325.°
Grease and flour 12 cup Bundt pan.
Sprinkle nuts over bottom of pan.
Mix all cake ingredients together.
Pour batter over nuts.

Bake 1 hour. Cool. Invert on serving plate.

Poke holes in cake.  Drizzle and smooth glaze evenly over top and sides.

Allow cake to absorb glaze and repeat until glaze is used up.

FOR GLAZE:
Melt butter in saucepan.

Stir in water and sugar.  Boil 5 minutes, stirring constantly.
Remove from heat. Stir in rum.

Optional: Decorate with whole maraschino cherries.

# Cherries in The Snow
## Carol Beebe

A make ahead dessert, pretty when served in a
crystal bowl or individual goblets.

## Ingredients

2 Cups whole milk
Dash of salt
½ Cup white rice
1 Envelope unflavored gelatin
¼ Cup milk
1/3 Cup sugar
½ Teaspoon vanilla extract
¼ Teaspoon almond extract
¼ Cup toasted slivered almonds
1 Cup heavy cream, whipped
1 Can or jar, 17 ounces, light or dark sweet
cherries
1 Tablespoon cornstarch
1 Tablespoon sherry wine

## Directions

Bring 2 cups milk and salt to boil.
Stir in rice. Cover and simmer for 20
minutes.

Soften gelatin in ¼ cup milk.

Add softened gelatin, sugar and extracts to rice mixture.  Cool until partially set.

Fold in almonds and whipped cream.

Pour into 6-cup crystal bowl or divide evenly among 6 goblets. Chill.

Drain cherries, reserving liquid, and arrange over gelatin mixture.

Combine reserved liquid with cornstarch.

Cook, stirring constantly, until thickened and smooth.

Add sherry.

Cool slightly. Spoon over cherries.

Refrigerate until serving.
Makes 6 servings.

# Snickerdoodles
## Betty Fontana

## Ingredients

1 Cup soft shortening (half butter)
2¾ Cups flour (sifted)
2 Teaspoons cream of tartar
1 Teaspoon baking soda
¼ Teaspoon salt
1½ Cups sugar plus
2 Tablespoons – reserved
2 Teaspoons of ground cinnamon
4 Eggs

## Directions

Preheat over to 400.°
Cream together butter, shortening, sugar and eggs.
Blend in the flour, cream of tartar, soda and salt. Shape dough by rounded spoonsful into balls.
Mix 2 tablespoons of sugar and the cinnamon and roll balls in the mixture.
Place 2 inches apart on ungreased baking sheets and bake 8 – 10 minutes.
Remove from baking sheets immediately.

# Apple Pie Bread Pudding
## Daisy Serle

## Ingredients

8 Cups bread – cubed and dried
(If you can leave bread cubes out for a few
hours so they get nice and dry. If not, just
place them on a baking sheet and bake them
at 350º for 10-15 minutes or until they're
dry but not toasted)
3 Medium apples, peeled, cored and
chopped
4 Eggs
1 Cup vanilla yogurt
1 Cup milk
2 Teaspoon cinnamon – divided
½ Teaspoon nutmeg
½ Cup sugar + 2 tablespoons
½ Cup raisins

SAUCE:
1 Cup Unsalted Butter
1 Cup Heavy Cream
1 Cup Brown Sugar

(Continued next page)

## INSTRUCTIONS

Preheat oven to 350°.

Spray a 9×13 baking dish with cooking spray.

In a large bowl, whisk together the yogurt, milk, eggs, 1 tsp cinnamon, nutmeg, and ½ cup sugar.

Stir in the apples, raisins, then gently fold in the bread cubes. Pour into the prepared pan.

In a small bowl, stir together 2 Tbsp sugar and 1 tsp cinnamon.

Sprinkle on top the bread pudding. Bake 30-40 minutes until puffed and golden brown.

While the bread pudding is baking, make the caramel sauce.

In a heavy saucepan over medium-low heat, stir together the butter, heavy cream, and brown sugar; bring to a boil.

Reduce heat to low, simmer until the sauce thickens. (about 5 minutes)

Pour over bread pudding to serve. Top with vanilla ice cream.

You can make this the night before and pop it in the oven for breakfast – it actually gets better if it sits overnight!

# Key Lime Cake
## Evelyn Fraley

## Ingredients

1 Box lemon cake mix
1 1/3 Cup veggie oil
4 Eggs
1 3-Ounce package lime Jello
¾ Cup orange juice

## Directions

Mix all ingredients and bake for
25 – 30 minutes at 350.°

## Icing

Cream together:
1 8-Ounce package cream cheese
3 Tablespoon fresh lime juice
4 Cups confection sugar
½ Cup butter and chopped nuts

# Grandma's Banana Pudding
## Daisy Serle

This is one of my grandchildren's favorites. I make it often.

## Ingredients

2 Bags Pepperidge Farm Chessmen cookies
6 to 8 Bananas – sliced
2 Cups milk
1 5-Ounce Box instant French vanilla pudding
1 8-Ounce package cream cheese, – softened
1 14-Ounce can sweetened condensed milk
1 12-Ounce container frozen whipped topping thawed or sweetened whipped cream

## Directions

Line the bottom of a 13 by 9 by 2-inch dish with 1 bag of cookies and layer bananas on top.
In a bowl, combine the milk and pudding mix and blend well using a handheld electric mixer.

Using another bowl, combine the cream cheese and condensed milk together and mix until smooth.

Fold the whipped topping into the cream cheese mixture.

Add the cream cheese mixture to the pudding mixture and stir until well blended. Pour the mixture over the cookies and bananas and cover with the remaining cookies.

Refrigerate until ready to serve.

# Strawberry-Almond Cream Tart
## Linda Williams

## Ingredients

CRUST: 35 honey graham crackers (9 sheets)
2 Tablespoons sugar
2 Tablespoons melted butter
4 Teaspoons water
Cooking spray
FILLING:
2/3 Cup (about 5 ounces) of 1/3 less-fat cream cheese
¼ Cup Sugar
½ Teaspoon Vanilla extract
¼ Teaspoon Almond extract
TOPPING:
6 Cups small fresh strawberries, – hulled and divided
2/3 Cup sugar
1 Tablespoons cornstarch
1 Teaspoon fresh lemon juice
2 Tablespoons sliced toasted almonds
Preheat oven to 350º

# Directions

CRUST:
To prepare crust, place crackers in a food processor or blender; process until crumbly. Add 2 tablespoons sugar, melted butter, and 4 teaspoons water; pulse just until moist. Place cracker mixture in a 9-inch round removable-bottom tart pan lightly coated with cooking spray, pressing into bottom and up sides of pan to ¾ inch.
Bake at 350° for 10 minutes, or until lightly browned.
Cool completely on a wire rack.

FILLING:
Combine cream cheese, ¼ cup sugar, and extracts in a medium bowl, stir until smooth. Spread cream cheese mixture evenly over bottom of tart shell.

TOPPING:
Place 2 cups strawberries in food processor or blender and blend until smooth. Combine strawberry puree, 2/3 cup sugar and cornstarch in a small saucepan over medium heat; stir with a whisk.

(Continued Next Page)

Bring to a boil, stirring constantly.
Reduce heat to low and cook 1 minute.

Remove glaze from heat.

Cool to room temperature stirring
occasionally.

Combine the remaining 4 cups strawberries
and juice, toss to coat.

Arrange berries, bottoms up, in a circular
pattern over filling.

Spoon half of glaze evenly over berries
(reserve remaining glaze for another use).
Sprinkle with toasted almonds.

# Southern Pecan Pie
## Vivian Shay

## Ingredients - Pie Crust

4 Cups all-purpose flour
1 Tablespoon sugar
2 Teaspoons salt
1 Egg
1¾ Cups Crisco shortening
1 Tablespoon vinegar
½ Cup water

## Pie Crust Directions

In medium size mixing bowl, with a fork, mix together flour, shortening, sugar and salt.
In a separate bowl beat, vinegar, egg and cold water.
Combine the 2 mixtures stirring with a fork until all ingredients are moistened. Mold dough into a ball with hands. Chill for at least 15 minutes before rolling into desired shape.

(continued next page)

169

Notes: May be left in refrigerator for up to 3 days.
May be frozen until ready to use. Will remain soft
in the refrigerator and can be taken out and rolled at
once. Enough for 2 (9 inch) double crust pies and 1
(9 inch) shell.

## Pie Ingredients

½ cup sugar
1 cup light corn syrup
1 Tablespoons all-purpose flour
¼ Teaspoon salt
2 Eggs
1 Teaspoon vanilla
1 Tablespoon melted butter
1 ¼ cup pecan halves
1 crust for 9-inch pie (unbaked)

## Pie Directions

Beat first 7 ingredients together until well
blended. Stir in pecans. Pour into pie pan,
lined with pastry. Bake in 300° oven for
about 1 hour.

# Crockpot Candy
## Daisy Serle

My friend Linda Williams loves this recipe.

## Ingredients

2 Pound white almond bark
4 Ounces German chocolate bar
12-Ounce bag semisweet chocolate chips
24 Ounces dry roasted peanuts

## Directions

Add all ingredients to slow cooker.
Let cook on low for 1 hour without messing
with it.
After an hour, stir to combine everything.
Allow to cook for another hour, stirring
every 15 minutes.
Drop spoonsful of the candy onto wax paper
and allow to cool completely.

# Grandma's Banana Bread
## Daisy Serle

## Ingredients

1 2/3 Cups all-purpose flour
1 Teaspoon baking soda
¼ Teaspoon ground cinnamon
½ Teaspoon salt
1 Cup plus 2 tablespoons sugar
2 Eggs
½ Cup oil
3½ Bananas, very ripe, mashed
2 Tablespoons creme fraiche or sour cream
1 Teaspoon vanilla extract
2/3 Cup walnuts, toasted and chopped
2/3 Cup dried cranberries

## Directions

Set oven to 350°.

Line the bottom of a loaf pan with parchment paper.

Sift together the flour, baking soda, cinnamon and salt.

Beat sugar and eggs with a whisk until light and fluffy, about 1 minute.

Drizzle in oil.

Add mashed bananas, creme fraiche, and vanilla.
Fold in dry ingredicnts cranberries, and nuts.

Pour into a lined loaf pan and bake for about 45 to 60 minutes.

# Yummy Pumpkin Cake
## Daisy Serle

## Ingredients

CAKE:
1 Package yellow cake mix
1 Egg
8 Tablespoons melted butter,
FILLING:
1 8-Ounce package cream cheese – softened
1 15-Ounce can pureed pumpkin
3 Eggs
1 Teaspoon vanilla extract
8 Tablespoons melted butter,
1 16-ounce Box powdered sugar
1 Teaspoon ground cinnamon
1 Teaspoon grated nutmeg
Topping –Fresh whipped cream

RECOMMENDED CANDY FOR
TOPPINGS
M and M's
Reese's pieces, crushed Snickers
Heath bars
Mini chocolates
Peanuts

# Directions

Preheat oven to 350.°

CAKE:
Combine the cake mix, egg and butter and mix well with an electric mixer. Mixture will be firm.

Pat batter into a 9x13inch pan

FILLING:
In a large bowl, beat the cream cheese and pumpkin until smooth with an electric mixer. Beat in eggs, vanilla and butter. Add the powdered sugar, cinnamon, nutmeg, and mix well.
Spread pumpkin mixture over cake batter in the pan and bake for about 40 minutes.
Make sure not to over bake as the center should be a little soft.
Let cool in the pans for 10 minutes before removing.

Serve with fresh whipped cream and candy topping.

## Brown Sugar Pound Cake

# Ann Hartnett

## Ingredients

1 Pound light brown sugar
1 Cup white sugar
1½ Cups shortening or butter
5 Large eggs
3 Cups flour
1 Cup milk
½ Teaspoon baking powder
½ Teaspoon salt
1 Teaspoon vanilla
1 Cup chopped nuts

Cream shortening, add sugar, then eggs beating well.

Sift dry ingredients together and add alternately with milk.
Then vanilla and nuts.

Pour into prepared tube pan and bake one hour at 325º to 350º depending on your oven.

# Lizzies
## Linda Williams

I made these cookies for our home tour and they were a big hit. The recipe freezes well.

## Ingredients

1 Cup butter.
1 Cup brown sugar – packed
4 Eggs
3 Tablespoon milk
1 Cup sherry or bourbon
3 Cups flour
3 Teaspoons baking soda
1 Teaspoon each ground cloves, nutmeg and cinnamon
1½ Pounds shelled pecans, chopped
1 Pound raisins – cut in half
1 Pound candied cherries, – cut up
½ Pound candied pineapple – cut up

## Directions

Cream butter and sugar.
Add eggs, milk and sherry; mix well.

(Continued next page)

Sift flour, soda and spices together several times; add to creamed mixture.

Add nuts, raisins and fruit; mix well. Drop by teaspoonfuls on greased cookie sheet.

Bake in 300° oven about 30 minutes. Yield: 200 Lizzies

# Eight-Layer Oreo Icebox Pie
## Daisy Serle

## Ingredients

1 Box Mint Oreo Cookies
1 Box regular Oreo Cookies
1 Oreo pie crust
1 8-Ounce block cream cheese – softened
1 Cup confectioners' sugar
1 14-Ounce Can sweetened condensed milk
1 Teaspoon vanilla extract
4 Ounces semisweet chocolate or chocolate chips
4 Ounces white chocolate or chocolate chips
Whipped cream and chocolate sauce for serving

## Instructions

In a large bowl beat the cream cheese, confectioners' sugar, condensed milk, and vanilla extract until light and voluminous. Set aside.

(Continued next page)

Arrange a layer of Mint Oreo cookies in the base of the Oreo cookie pie crust. Cover it with half of the cream cheese mixture just until you can see the cookies.

Melt the semisweet chocolate in the microwave and stir until smooth. Spread the melted chocolate in an even layer over the top of the cream cheese mixture.

Arrange a layer of regular Oreo cookies on top of the melted chocolate. Cover them with the remaining half of the cream cheese mixture.

Place 5 Mint Oreo cookies and 5 regular Oreo cookies in a freezer bag and lightly crush them with a rolling pin. Scatter the top over the cream cheese mixture.

In the microwave melt the white chocolate and stir until smooth. Drizzle over the top of the crushed Oreos. Freeze the pie for 4 hours, or until solid.

Serve with whipped cream and chocolate sauce!

# Old Fashioned Spice Carrot Cake
## Linda Williams

There is no need to put a cream cheese frosting on this. It calls for a glaze, but the flavor of the cake stands on its own. I prefer it without a glaze, so I am not including it. This is one of my favorite cakes.

## Ingredients

1½ Cups Salad oil
2½ Cups granulated sugar
4 Eggs yolks
5 Tablespoons hot water
2 Cups sifted all-purpose flour
1½ Teaspoons double-acting baking powder
½ Teaspoon baking soda
¼ Teaspoon salt
1 Teaspoon nutmeg
1 Teaspoon cinnamon
1 Teaspoon ground cloves
1 ¾ Cups grated raw carrots
1 Cup chopped pecans
4 Egg whites

(Continued next page)

## Directions

Heat oven to 350.º
Grease well, then flour a 10-inch Bundt cake pan.
In a large bowl, with electric mixer at medium speed, cream oil and sugar until well blended.
Then beat in egg yolks, one at a time, beating well after each addition.
Now beat in the hot water.
Sift together flour, baking powder, baking soda, salt, nutmeg, cinnamon and cloves, and beat into egg mixture.
Now stir in 1½ cups of grated carrots, then pecans.
Next beat egg whites until soft peaks form and fold into batter.
Turn into prepared pan and bake 60 to 70 minutes or until a cake tester inserted into the center of cake comes out clean.
Cool in pan 15 minutes, then remove from pan and finish cooling on wire rack.

Cake keeps well when wrapped and refrigerated or frozen.

# Microwave Baked Apples
## Pat Bankhead

## Ingredients

2 Apples (I use Fiji)
2 Tablespoons brown sugar
1 Teaspoon nutmeg
1 Teaspoon cinnamon
2 Teaspoons butter

## Directions

Optional – dried Craisins and chopped walnuts

I cut apples in half and core center.
Mix other ingredients together.
Stuff center of apple with mixture.
Place apples in a deep casserole dish and cover. Microwave 3 ½ to 4 minutes or until tender.

Let sit for a couple minutes before serving. Can top with ice cream.

# Jiffy Coconut Pie
## A Quick Dessert
## Pat Bankhead

## Ingredients

¾ Stick butter
3 Eggs, slightly beaten
1¼ Cups sugar
2 Tablespoons self-rising flour
1 Tablespoon vanilla
1 Large can carnation milk
1 3½-Ounce can or 1 1/3 cups coconut (I add a package or two of the thawed frozen coconut from the freezer section at grocery.)

## Directions

Melt butter and add sugar. Beat eggs. Pour in and stir.
Add flour and stir in vanilla, milk, and coconut. Place in greased (butter) pie plate. Cook at 350° about 30 minutes or until set in the middle and golden brown.

# Turtle Cake
## Pat Bankhead

## Ingredients

1 Box German chocolate or Devil's food cake mix
½ Cup milk
1 14-Ounce package caramels – about 50 caramels
½ Stick margarine or butter, melted
1 6-Ounce package semisweet chocolate chips
½ Cup chopped pecans

## Directions

Prepare cake mix as directed on box.
Pour half the cake mixture into greased and floured 13 X 9 pan. Bake at 350º for 15 minutes or until toothpick inserted in center comes out clean. Turn oven to 250.º

In heavy saucepan mix milk, butter, and caramels and cook over low heat until caramel is melted.

(Continued next page)

Pour caramel
mixture over
cake.

On top of
caramel mixture
sprinkle the
pecans and
chocolate chips.

Pour remaining cake batter on top.
Bake at 250º for 20 minutes then at 350º for
10 minutes.

Cool, cut into squares.

Serve with whipped cream if desired.

# Oreo Cookie Pie
## Ann Hartnett

## Ingredients

1 Bag Oreo cookies and 1 or 2 sticks butter
1 8-Ounce package cream cheese
12 Ounces cool whip
Large package instant chocolate pudding
mix in 2½ Cups whole milk.
Cool whip on top

## Directions

CRUST:
Crush Oreos. (Save a little for the topping)
Melt butter and mix with oreos.  Press into
bottom 9x13 pan.  Chill.
FILLING:
Mix 8 ounces cream cheese and ½ of 12-
ounce cool whip.
Spread on chilled crust.  Mix 1 large
pudding and 2 or 2½ cups whole milk.
Spread on cheese mixture.
Top with rest of cool whip and some
crushed Oreos.

# Carrot Cake
## Pat Bankhead

## Ingredients

3 Eggs
2 Cups sugar
1½ Cups vegetable oil
2 Teaspoons vanilla extract
2 Cups flour
2 Teaspoon baking soda
2 Teaspoon cinnamon
1 Teaspoon salt
2 Large carrots coarsely grated (I used 4 smaller carrots.)
1½ Cups pineapple, unsweetened, chopped and drained (I used 20 ounce can crushed pineapple, drained)
1 Cup chopped pecans
3½ Ounces flaked coconut, optional (I omitted)

## Directions

Preheat oven 350.º
Beat eggs, add sugar, oil and vanilla.
In a small bowl, sift flour, baking soda, cinnamon, and salt,

Combine flour mixture with the egg mixture.

Add carrots, pineapple and pecans, in that order. Beat until thoroughly mixed. Pour batter into a greased 9 X 13 pan. Bake 50 minutes. (a little longer if needed) Cool.

CREAM CHEESE FROSTING:
I used the following frosting recipe, not the one attached to the cake recipe.
1 stick butter
1 Box powdered sugar, sifted
1 8-Ounce package cream cheese
2 Teaspoons vanilla

# German-Chocolate Cake
## Pat Bankhead

## Cake Ingredients

1 4-ounce package Bakers German Sweet baking chocolate
½ Cup water
2 Cups flour
1 Teaspoon baking soda
¼ Teaspoon salt
1 Cup (2 sticks) butter
2 Cups sugar
4 Egg yolks
1 Teaspoon vanilla
1 Cup buttermilk
4 Egg whites

## Cake Directions

Microwave chocolate and water in large bowl on high for 1½ to 2 minutes or until chocolate is almost melted, stirring halfway through heating time.

Stir until chocolate is completely melted. Mix flour, baking soda and salt. Set aside.

Beat butter and sugar in large bowl with electric mixer on medium speed until light and fluffy. Add egg yolks, 1 at a time, beating well after each addition.

Stir in chocolate mixture and vanilla. Add flour mixture alternately with buttermilk, beating after each addition until smooth.

Beat egg whites in another large bowl with electric mixer on high speed until stiff peaks form.
Gently stir into batter.
Pour into prepared pans. Bake 30 minutes or until cake springs back when lightly touched in center. Immediately run spatula between cakes and sides of pans.

Cool 15 minutes; remove from pans.
Remove wax paper.
Cool completely on wire racks.

Spread Coconut-Pecan Filling and Frosting between layers and over top of cake.
Makes 12 servings.
Note: This delicate cake will have a slightly sugary top crust which tends to crack,

(Continued next page)

# Frosting Ingredients

Coconut-Pecan Filling and Frosting
1½ Cups sugar.
1 12-ounce can evaporated milk
¾ Cup (1½ sticks) butter
4 Egg yolks, slightly beaten
1½ Teaspoon vanilla
1 7-Ounce package (about 21/3 cups)
coconut
1½ Cups chopped pecans

# Frosting Directions

Stir milk, sugar, butter, egg yolks, and
vanilla in large saucepan.
Stirring constantly, cook on medium heat 12
minutes or until thickened and golden
brown. Remove from heat. Stir in coconut
and pecans. Cool to room temperature and
of spreading consistency. Makes about 4 ½
cups.

# Lemon Icebox Cake
## Vivian Shay

## Ingredients

8 Ounces Cool Whip
2 pkg. lemon instant pudding
1 Package Graham crackers
½ Cup butter
2 Tablespoons milk
2 Tablespoons lemon juice
1 Cup powdered sugar

## Directions

Mix together until thick – 8 oz. cool whip
and 2 packages of lemon instant Pudding

Line bottom of pan with graham crackers.
Spread lemon mixture.
Layer of graham crackers
Spread lemon mixture
Layer of graham crackers.

(Continued next page)

# Frosting Directions

Mix ½ cup butter, 2 tablespoons milk,
2 tablespoons lemon juice and 1 cup
powdered sugar.

Frost the cake.

Freeze 4 hours.

Serve with fresh raspberries (optional)

# Apple Pound Cake
## Ann Hartnett

## Ingredients

1½ Cup corn oil
2 Cups sugar
3 Cups flour
3 eggs
1 Teaspoon salt
1 Teaspoon baking soda
1 Teaspoon cinnamon
1 Teaspoon vanilla
3 Cups diced eating apples
1 Cup chopped nuts

## Directions

Mix as for any cake.
Add apples and nuts.
Bake for 2 hours 15 minutes in a tube pan at
300.º

You may put lemon glaze on top while cake
is hot

(Continued next page)

## LEMON GLAZE INGREDIENTS

Juice of 2 lemons
1 Cup powdered sugar
Rum to taste

## GLAZE DIRECTIONS

Melt butter and slowly stir in confectioners' sugar.

Add rum and heat until bubbly.

# Carrot Cake
# Ann Hartnett

## Ingredients

CAKE:
2¼ cups Pillsbury's Best all-purpose flour
4 Cups sugar
2 Teaspoon soda
1 Teaspoon cinnamon
¼ Teaspoon salt
2 Cups (medium) shredded carrots
1½ Cups oil
4 Eggs
1 Cup chopped nuts

FROSTING:
3 Cups powdered sugar
2 Tablespoons margarine or butter softened
1 Teaspoon vanilla
8-Ounce package cream cheese

## Directions

Heat oven to 350.°
Grease (not oil) and lightly flour two 9-inch
round cake pans.

(Continued next page)

In large bowl blend all cake ingredients except nuts at low speed until moistened. Beat 3 minutes at high speed.

Stir in nuts.
Pour batter into prepared pans.

Bake at 350° for 35-45 minutes or until toothpick inserted in center comes out clean.

Cool completely.

In medium bowl blend frosting ingredients and beat until smooth. Spread over cake.

Tip – *Cake may be baked in 13x9 inch pan; grease on bottom only. Bake 40-45 minutes.*

# Applesauce Snack Cake
## Ann Hartnett

## Ingredients

CAKE:
½ Cup margarine or butter
¾ Cup Pillsbury's Best all-purpose flour
¾ Cup Pillsbury's Best medium rye or whole wheat flour
¾ Cup firmly packed brown sugar
½ Cup raisins or chopped dates
1 Teaspoon baking soda
2 Teaspoons cinnamon
½ Teaspoon salt
1 Cup applesauce
1 Egg

TOPPING
½ Cup firmly packed brown sugar
½ Cup chopped nuts
¼ Cup Pillsbury's Best medium rye or whole wheat flour
¼ Cup softened margarine or butter

(Continued next page)

## Directions

Heat oven to 350.º
Generously grease (not oil) and lightly flour 9-inch square pan.

In medium saucepan melt margarine or butter. Remove from heat.

Stir in remaining cake ingredients and blend well.

Pour batter into prepared pan.
In small bowl combine Topping ingredients until crumbly.

Sprinkle over batter.

Bake at 350º for 30-35 minutes or until a toothpick inserted in center comes out clean.

# Fran's So Good Cookies
## Fran Huntress

## Ingredients

1 Stick of margarine or butter
1 Cup oil
1 Cup white sugar
1 Egg
1 Cup brown sugar
1 Teaspoon vanilla
1 Cup crushed corn flakes
1 Cup oatmeal
½ Cup flaked coconut
1 Cup chopped pecans
3½ Cups flour
1 Teaspoon baking soda
1 Teaspoon salt
Sprinkles

## Directions

Pre-heat oven to 375.°
Mix well together – oil, margarine or butter, brown sugar, white sugar, egg and vanilla.

(Continued next page)

Mix and add the crushed corn flakes, oatmeal, chopped coconut and chopped nuts

Mix and add to above, flour, salt and baking soda.

Drop teaspoons of mixture on ungreased cookie sheet. Press down with a fork.  Add some sprinkles.

Bake 8-10 minutes at 375.° Makes about 4 dozen.

*Fran Huntress spent a lot of time making these cookies, not because they are difficult to make (they're not), but because everyone loved them.*

# BLUEBERRY BUCKLE
## Rosemarie Galloway

As a military spouse for 27 years, this delicious cake was standard fare at morning neighborhood gatherings.

## Cake Ingredients

2 Cups of all-purpose flour plus
2 Tablespoons of flour for dusting blueberries
¼ Teaspoon salt
¾ Cup sugar
2 Teaspoons baking powder
1 Stick of butter softened
1 Large egg
½ Cup milk
16 Ounces blueberries (pint)

## Streusel Topping Ingredients

¼ Cup softened butter
½ Cup sugar
1/3 Cup all-purpose flour
½ Teaspoon cinnamon
¼ Cup chopped walnuts

(Continued next page)

# Directions

Heat oven to 350.°

Butter an 8-inch springform pan.

Whisk together the two cups of flour, the baking powder and the salt in a medium bowl.

In a separate bowl, beat together the butter and sugar until creamy and then beat in the egg.

Add the flour mixture in 3 parts, alternating with the milk.

Toss the blueberries with the remaining 2 tablespoons of flour and fold in gently*. Combine ingredients for the streusel topping. Sprinkle this over the batter.

Bake for 60 minutes.

When the cake has cooled, run a knife around the edge of the pan and unsnap side of pan and lift the cake out.

* Tossing the blueberries in flour prevent them from sinking to the bottom of the pan.

# Apple Dapple Cake
## Marlene Wells

## Ingredients

3 Eggs
1½ Cup oil
2 Cups sugar
2 Teaspoon vanilla
2 Cups flour
1 Teaspoon salt
1 Teaspoon soda
2 Cups chopped apples
1½ Cups chopped walnuts
1½ Cups golden raisins

## Directions

Mix eggs, oil, vanilla and sugar.  Blend well.
Sift together flour, salt, and soda. And add
to first mixture.
Fold in apples, raisins and nuts.
Pour into tube pan.
Bake 1 hour at 350.º

(Continued next page)

SAUCE:
1 (Packed) cup brown sugar
¼ cup milk
¾ Cup butter

Mix and cook three minutes after it begins to
gently boil – stirring constantly.
Pour over hot cake while cake is in pan.

Let cake cool completely before removing.

# Grandma W's Cookies
## Roz McClure

## Ingredients

½ Cup butter
1¾ Cups flour
1 Cup sugar
2 Teaspoons baking powder
1 Egg
½ Teaspoons salt
Pecan halves
2 Teaspoons-vanilla

## Directions

Cream butter and sugar.
Add egg and cream again – well.
Add flour, salt, baking powder and vanilla.
Mix.
Shape into 2-inch rolls.
Chill.
Slice thin.
Press nut half on each cookie.
Bake at 425.° Around 8 minutes.

# Sour Cream Coffee Cake
## Pat Bankhead

## Ingredients

1 Stick butter
1 Cup sugar
2 Eggs
2 Cups flour
1 Teaspoon baking powder
1 Teaspoon soda
½ Teaspoon salt
1 Cup sour cream
1 Teaspoon almond flavoring

TOPPING:
½ Cup brown sugar
½ Cup white sugar
1½ Teaspoon cinnamon

## Directions

Cream butter and sugar. Add eggs. Beat well.
Mix next 4 dry ingredients together and add alternately with sour cream.
Add almond flavoring. Mix.

Spread ½ of the mixture in a greased 9 X 13 pan.

Combine topping ingredients and sprinkle ½ of the topping mixture over the cake mixture.

Add second ½ of the cake mixture and top with the topping mixture.

Bake 325° for 40 minutes.

# Apple Dumplings
## Marilyn Barnini

## Ingredients

2 Cans crescent rolls
2 Sticks butter
1 Teaspoon cinnamon
4 granny smith apples, peeled, cored and
quartered
1½ Cups sugar
12 Ounce can Mountain Dew soda, room
temperature

## Directions

Wrap each quarter of apple in triangle of
crescent roll, starting with large end. (It will
not cover all of the apples but will as it
bakes).
Put in 13x9 inch dish. Melt the butter, add
sugar and cinnamon. Cook until well
blended.
Pour over apples, then pour can of Mountain
Dew over all.
Bake at 350° for 40-50 minutes until golden
brown. Let sit a few minutes to thicken.

# Berry Angel Delight
## Marilyn Barnini

## Ingredients

1 Cup whipping cream
1 Tablespoon sugar
2 Cups Yoplait thick and creamy vanilla yogurt
1 Round angel food cake cut into 1-inch pieces
½ Pint fresh blueberries
½ Pint fresh raspberries
1 Cup fresh strawberries – quartered

## Directions

In medium bowl, beat whipping cream and sugar with electric mixer on high speed until stiff peaks form.

Fold in yogurt.

In large bowl place cake pieces and fold in yogurt mixture.

In medium bowl, gently mix berries together. (Continued next page)

Spoon half of the cake mixture into 9-inch springform pan; press firmly in pan with rubber spatula.

Top with half of the berries.

Repeat with remaining cake mixture; press with spatula.

Top with berries.

Cover and refrigerate at least 4 hours or overnight.

Run metal spatula carefully along the side of dessert to loosen; remove side of pan.

Cut dessert into wedges.

# Dump Cake
## Marilyn Barnini

## Ingredients

1 Package yellow cake mix
1 20-Ounce can crushed pineapple, undrained
1 21-Ounce can cherry pie filling
1 Cup pecans – chopped
1 Stick melted butter
Optional toppings – whipped cream or maraschino cherries

## Directions

Oven at 350.°

Grease a 13x9 inch pan.

Dump the undrained pineapple into pan.

Spread it evenly.

Spread the cherry pie filling on top.

Sprinkle the dry cake mix over the cherry layer. (Continued next page)

Sprinkle pecans over the cake mix.

Drizzle the butter on top.

Spread it evenly.

Bake for 35-45 minutes.

Serve warm or cooled with whipped cream
and cherries.

# Apple Crisp
## Pat Bankhead

## Ingredients

4 Cups sliced pared tart apples (about 4 medium)
2/3 to ¾ cup brown sugar (packed)
½ Cup all-purpose flour
½ Cup oats
¾ Teaspoon cinnamon
¾ Teaspoon nutmeg
1/3 Cup butter or margarine – softened

## Directions

Heat oven to 375.º
Grease square pan, 8x8x2.
Place apple slices in pan.
Mix remaining ingredients thoroughly.
Sprinkle over apples.
Bake 30 minutes or until apples are tender and topping is golden brown.
Serve warm and, if desired, with light cream or ice cream.

# Coke Cake
## Ann Hartnett

## Ingredients

2 Cups sugar
2 Cups all-purpose flour.
½ Cup butter
3 Tablespoon cocoa
½ Cup Crisco oil
1 Cup Coke
1 Teaspoon baking soda (in buttermilk)
½ Cup buttermilk
2 Eggs,
1 Teaspoon vanilla
1½ Cups miniature marshmallows.

## Directions

Mix this cake by hand.

In a large bowl sift together 2 cups sugar
and 2 cups all-purpose flour.
Mix in saucepan ½ cup butter, 3 tablespoons
cocoa, ½ cup Crisco oil and 1 cup of Coke.
Bring to a boil and pour over dry mixture.

Mix 1 teaspoon baking soda in buttermilk then add 2 eggs, 1 teaspoon vanilla and 1½ cups miniature marshmallows.
Mix all together and pour into well-greased 9x13pan.
Bake at 350° for 45 minutes.

ICING FOR COKE CAKE:

## Ingredients

½ Cup butter
6 Tablespoons Coke
3 Tablespoons cocoa
1 Box powdered sugar
1 Teaspoon Vanilla
1 Cup nuts

## Directions

Mix butter and coke in a saucepan and heat to a boil.
Remove from stove and add 1 box powdered sugar (a little at a time).
Then stir in 1 teaspoon vanilla and 1 cup nuts. Hand mix and spread over hot cake.

# Chocolate Chip Peanut Butter Bars
## Vivian Shay

## Ingredients

BASE AND TOPPING:
2½ cups quick-cooking rolled oats
1¼ cups firmly packed brown sugar
1 Cup all-purpose flour
½ Teaspoon baking soda
1 Cup softened butter
FILLING:
1 14-Ounce can sweet condensed milk (not evaporated)
¼ Cup peanut butter
½ Teaspoon vanilla
1 6-Ounce package (1 cup) semi-sweet chocolate chips
½ Cup coarsely chopped salted peanuts

## Directions

Heat oven to 350.°

Spray 13x9 inch pan with nonstick cooking spray.

218

In large bowl combine all base and topping ingredients, mix at low speed until crumbly. (Reserve 2 cups of crumb mixture for topping)

Press remaining crumb mixture in bottom of sprayed pan to form base.

In small bowl combine condensed milk, peanut butter and vanilla, mix until well blended.

Pour mixture evenly over base.

Sprinkle with chocolate chips and peanuts.

Sprinkle reserved crumb mixture over top; press down gently.

Bake at 350° for 25-30 minutes or until golden brown.

Center will not be set.

Cool 1 hour 15 minutes or until completely cooled.  Cut into 36 bars.

# BREADS AND BREAKFASTS

# BREADS AND BREAKFASTS
## TABLE OF CONTENTS

# Zucchini Bread
## Linda Williams

## Ingredients

1 Cup oil
2 Cups sugar
3 Eggs
2 Cups shredded zucchini
3 Cups flour
3 Teaspoons cinnamon
1 Teaspoon baking soda
½ Teaspoon baking powder

## Directions

Combine all ingredients.

Bake at 325° for 1 hour.

Makes 2 loaves.

# Grits Breakfast Casserole
## Pat Bankhead

## Ingredients

2 Pounds bulk sausage
1 Cup cooked grits,
2 Cups sharp cheddar cheese
5 Eggs
1½ Cups milk
½ Stick butter
Salt and pepper to taste

## Directions

Brown and drain sausage and crumble in bottom of 9 X 13 greased casserole.

Cook grits according to package directions (stiff is better than runny).

Add butter and cheese to cooked grits.

Beat eggs, milk, salt, and pepper together and add to slightly cooled grits mixture.

Pour over
sausage in
casserole.

Bake at 350° for
1 hour. This can
be done ahead
and frozen.

Freeze
uncooked.

Thaw in refrigerator and bake according to
directions. Recipe can be halved.

# Basic Tropical Jelly
## Vivian Shay

## Ingredients

Fruit – About 4 cups.
Under-ripe fruit – about half a cup
Water – To cover fruit
Sugar – equal to juice produced

## Directions

In 2-3-quart saucepan, put ripe fruit to no
more than halfway to sides. Add a handful
of under-ripe fruit.
Cover fruit with water. Boil until fruit is soft
and you can either strain, mash or sieve it.
Pour pulp into jelly bag and let drip.

(NOTE: Some can be squeezed and others
will form a cloudy jelly if squeezed)

Measure equal amount of juice and sugar,
but do not cook too much at one time. (If
you start out with the ½ saucepan of fruit,
you will have the right amount to cook at
one time.)

Bring sugar-juice mixture to boil.

Cook until jelly stage is reached.

Pour into sterile jars and seal.

TROPICAL JELLY NOTE:  Above can be used for:  Berry jelly, Loquat jelly – (if too sweet add lime juice).  Surinam Cherry jelly (wild FLA cherry), Pitomba jelly and Governor's Plum jelly – bag can be squeezed for these fruits.

# Holiday French Toast
## Daisy Serle

One of my family's favorite meals. I make it the day before
holidays like Thanksgiving and Christmas. Pop it in the oven
in the morning and, voila, breakfast is ready.

## INGREDIENTS

¼ Cup (4 Tablespoons) butter, melted
¾ Cup packed light brown sugar
1 Loaf brioche or challah (a French bread
loaf can a used) sliced into 1½ inch slices
8 Eggs, slightly beaten
1 Cup whole milk
1 Tablespoon vanilla extract
1 Teaspoon ground cinnamon
¼ Teaspoon ground ginger
½ Cup pecans, measured then chopped
1 Teaspoon salt

Optional – maple syrup and powdered sugar
topping

## DIRECTIONS

In a small bowl combine brown sugar and
melted butter and pour on the bottom of a
9x13 baking dish.

Arrange slices of bread in the baking dish overlapping if necessary.

Combine milk, eggs, vanilla, salt, cinnamon, and ginger in a bowl and pour evenly over bread slices.

Sprinkle chopped pecans over bread slices.

Wrap tightly with plastic wrap and place in the refrigerator for 4-12 hours.
In the morning, take the casserole out of the fridge for at least 10 minutes while you are preheating your oven to 350.°

Bake casserole for 30-35 minutes.
If top starts browning too quickly place a foil loosely over the top of the casserole for the last 10 minutes or so. You want it to cook long enough to make sure the bottom part is cooked but don't dry it out completely.

Remove casserole from oven and let it cool slightly before serving. Serve with a dusting of powdered sugar and a drizzle of maple syrup.

# Herb and Onion Bread
## Bill Serle
Makes two loaves

## Ingredients

4 Cups tepid water
¼ cup active dry yeast
4 Teaspoons salt
1 Teaspoon dried dill weed
1 Teaspoon fresh rosemary
6 Tablespoons sugar
¼ Cup melted butter
½ Cup powdered milk
1 Cup chopped onions
6-7 Cups all-purpose white flour
4 Cups Whole-wheat flour

## Directions

Makes two 9 x 5 x 3 loaves.

Mix with a whisk: water, yeast, salt, dill, rosemary, sugar, butter, powdered milk, and onions.

Allow yeast to activate until mixture becomes bubbly. (10-15 minutes)

Add flours to yeast mixture.

Beat by hand until well-mixed. Turn dough onto floured surface and knead for 10 minutes. If you have a dough hook and mixer, beat for 5 minutes on low speed.

Allow mixture to rise until doubled in size, (45 minutes)

After dough rises, place on lightly floured surface and knead well. (Knead about 30-35 times, adding flour as needed)

Shape into two equal-sized loaves and place in buttered 9" loaf pans.

Let the pans rest for about 10 minutes before baking.

Bake loaves at 350º for 45-55 minutes. Allow loaves to cool in pan briefly then remove from pans to finish cooling.

While loaves are still warm brush with your favorite salted butter.
Enjoy!!

# Cranberry Zucchini Bread
## Daisy Serle

## Ingredients

3¼ Cups all-purpose flour plus
1 Tablespoon – separated
2 Teaspoons cinnamon
½ Teaspoon ground ginger
1½ Teaspoons baking powder
½ Teaspoons baking soda
½ Teaspoons salt
2 Eggs
1 Teaspoon Vanilla
1 Cup sugar
½ Cup brown sugar
½ Cup vegetable oil
Juice and zest of 2 medium Oranges
2 Cups finely shredded, unpeeled zucchinis
1 Cup dried cranberries

## Directions

Preheat the oven to 350° and grease two
baking pans,.

Line the bottoms with baking paper, then
grease the paper.

In a bowl, sift together the flour, cinnamon, ginger, baking powder, baking soda, and salt.

In another bowl, beat together the eggs, vanilla, sugars, oil and orange peel.

Gradually add the flour mixture to the creamed mixture, alternating with the orange juice, mixing just enough to combine after each addition.

In a small bowl toss the cranberries together with the 1 tbsp of flour, to coat them. Stir in the zucchini and the floured cranberries, then pour the mixture into the prepared baking pans.

Bake for about 55 minutes, or until a toothpick test comes out clean, let cool in pans for about 10 minutes before removing to wire racks to cool completely.

# Snickerdoodle Bread
## Daisy Serle

## Bread Ingredients

1 Cup of unsalted butter softened
1 Cup sugar
¼ Cup light brown sugar (packed)
½ Teaspoon salt
2 Teaspoons ground cinnamon
2 Large Eggs
1 Tablespoon vanilla extract
¾ Cup sour cream
1½ Cups all-purpose flour
1 Teaspoon baking powder
2 Tablespoons of flour to dredge the chocolate chips
1 Cup mini chocolate or cinnamon chips

## Directions

Preheat oven to 350° and grease a large loaf pan.
In a medium bowl, cream together the butter, sugar, salt, and cinnamon.
Add in the eggs, vanilla, and sour cream.
Add in the flour and baking powder stirring until just combined.

Fold in the dredged chocolate chips.
Pour batter (it will be thick) into the
prepared loaf pans, filling about 2/3 full.

## Topping Ingredients
3 Tablespoons Sugar
2 Teaspoons ground cinnamon

## Topping Directions

In a small bowl, combine sugar and ground
cinnamon.

Sprinkle mixture evenly on top of batter.

Place pan in oven and bake 30-35 minutes if
mini loaves, or 60-65 minutes in large loaf
pans.

Remove from oven
and allow to cool
slightly before
removing from pan
and serving!

# Apple Fritter Pull Apart Bread
## Daisy Serle

## Ingredients

2 Cans refrigerated biscuits such as Grands

FOR THE FILLING:
4 apples, peeled, cored, and very finely diced
1 teaspoon lemon juice
2/3 cup brown sugar, lightly packed
¼ Cup granulated sugar
1 Teaspoon vanilla extract
1 Teaspoon ground cinnamon
½ Teaspoon ground nutmeg
¼ Teaspoon ground ginger
¼ Teaspoon ground allspice

FOR THE GLAZE:
1½ cups powdered sugar
¼ cup half and half, or more as needed
1 teaspoon vanilla

# Directions

Add all of the filling ingredients to a large saucepan over medium heat.

Cook, stirring occasionally, until the apples have browned and softened, and the sauce has thickened, about 8-10 minutes. Set aside to cool.

Preheat the oven to 350.° Spray a 9 x 5 inch loaf pan with cooking spray.

Using a paring knife, cut each biscuit in half horizontally to make 32 rounds (you should be able to cut them slightly and then pull them apart the rest of the way).

Flatten each biscuit half with your hand to thin them out.

One at a time, spoon about a tablespoon of the apple filling onto each biscuit half, and then stack the biscuit halves on top of one another to form stacks of four with filling in between.

(Continued next page)

Place the stacks in the loaf pan, arranging so that no filling touches the edges of the pan.

Repeat until the pan is full – leave room for the biscuits to expand while baking). You may not need to use all of the biscuits.

Cover with aluminum foil and bake for 40 minutes.

Then, remove the aluminum foil and bake until golden brown and cooked through, checking every 5-10 minutes.

Let the loaf cool for 5 minutes and then remove from the pan.

GLAZE: Whisk together the powdered sugar and half and half, adding more, if necessary, to reach the desired consistency.

Add the vanilla and whisk again until well-combined. Drizzle liberally over fritter loaf. Serve warm.

# Pineapple Jam
## Vivian Shay

## Ingredients

Pineapples
Sugar

## Directions

Peel, grate or chop as many pineapples as
desired.
Weigh and allow 1 pound of sugar to 1
pound of pineapple.
Mix sugar and pineapple well.
Put in cool place overnight.

In morning place pot on stove and cook
mixture for ½ hour, or until soft enough to
push through sieve.
Put through coarse sieve.
Return to pot and continue cooking, stirring
constantly for about ½ hour or until a clear
amber stage is reached.

Put into sterile jars and seal.

# Pumpkin Bread
## Monica Fischer

## Ingredients

3½ Cups flour
3 Cups sugar
2 Teaspoon baking soda
1½ Teaspoon salt
1 Teaspoon cinnamon
1 Teaspoon nutmeg
¾ Cup oil
2/3 Cup water
4 Eggs
1 14-Ounce can solid packed pumpkin

## Directions

Mix all dry ingredients in large bowl.

Mix all wet ingredients except pumpkin.

Combine wet and dry ingredients and mix well.
Add pumpkin and stir until well blended.

Pour into 4 loaf pans and bake at 350° for 1 hour. Enjoy!

# Mango Nut Bread
## Carol Beebe

## Ingredients

2 Cups all-purpose flour
1½ Cups sugar
1 Teaspoon baking soda
½ Teaspoon salt
½ Teaspoon ground cinnamon
3 Eggs
½ Cup vegetable oil
1 Teaspoon vanilla extract
2 Cups chopped mangoes
½ Cup chopped dates
½ Cup chopped walnuts or macadamia nuts

## Directions

In a large bowl, combine the first five
ingredients.
In another bowl, beat eggs, oil and vanilla. Stir
into dry ingredients just until moistened. Fold in
mangoes, dates and nuts (batter will be stiff).
Spoon into two greased 8x4-in. loaf pans. Bake
at 350° for 50-55 minutes or until a toothpick
inserted in the center comes out clean.
Cool for 10 minutes before removing from pans
to wire racks.

# Strawberry Muffins
## Carol Scott

## Ingredients

3 Cups flour
2 Cups sugar
1 Tablespoon cinnamon
1 Teaspoon baking soda
1 Teaspoon salt
2 Cups frozen strawberries, thawed, undrained
1 Cup vegetable oil
3 Eggs beaten
½ Cup chopped pecans

## Directions

In large bowl combine flour, sugar, cinnamon, baking soda and salt.
In another bowl mix strawberries, oil and eggs.

Stir into dry ingredients until just moistened.

Fold in pecans.

Fill greased muffins cups ¾ full.

Bake at 375° for 15-18 minutes or until muffins test done.

Cool for 10 minutes before removing from pan to a wire rack to cool completely.

FREEZE OPTION: Securely wrap and freeze cooled muffins in plastic wrap and foil. Thaw at room temperature to use.

# Artichoke Cheese Bread
## Linda Williams

## Ingredients

2 Loaves of French bread
½ cup butter
6 medium cloves crushed garlic
1½ Cups sour cream
2 Cups grated mozzarella
½ Cup parmesan cheese
2 Tablespoons parsley
1 Cup grated cheddar
1 14-Ounce can artichokes, drained and chopped

## Directions

Cut bread lengthwise and hollow out both sides.

Save the bread you removed and cut into small pieces.

Melt butter over low heat and add the saved hollowed-out bread pieces. Cook until golden.

Stir in garlic and heat a bit more.  Remove
from heat.

Add sour cream, mozzarella, and parmesan
cheeses.  Stir in parsley and cheddar.  Fold
in artichokes.

Spoon mixture into bread shells.

Top with remaining mozzarella.

Bake at 350° for 25-30 minutes.

Let stand 5 minutes before serving.

# Beer Bread
## Gail Holder

## Ingredients

3½ cups all-purpose flour
1 Tablespoon baking powder
12 Ounces beer
3 Tablespoons sugar
1½ Teaspoon salt
1 egg, beaten

## Directions

Adjust oven rack to lower middle position
and heat oven to 375.º
Mix flour, sugar, baking powder & salt in
large bowl.
Add beer (no sips) and stir with a fork until
just combined.
Turn dough onto a floured surface.
Knead quickly to form a ball.
Place bread on baking sheet and confidently
slit an "X" on top with a serrated knife.
Brush loaf with egg wash.
Bake until golden brown, about 45 minutes.
Transfer to wire rack to cool.
Yield 12.

# Cheese Biscuits
## Betty Fontana

## Ingredients

½ Pound real butter
½ Pound New York State sharp cheese
2 Heaping cups flour
¼ Teaspoon red pepper

## Directions

Soften butter, add grated cheese and flour.

Roll in wax paper and store in refrigerator.

Slice in ¼ inch slices and bake on cookie sheet at 450° for about 10-12 minutes.

# BANANA BREAD
## Pat Bankhead
I doubled the original recipe

## Ingredients

3½ Cups flour
2 Teaspoons teaspoon baking powder
1 Teaspoon soda
11/3 Cups brown sugar
2/3 Cup Mazola oil (I use any canola oil)
4 Eggs
1 Cup nuts – optional
4 to 5 Mashed bananas

## Directions

Combine first 7 ingredients. (I sift all dry ingredients together then add oil and eggs.)

Add mashed bananas to the mixture.

Pour into greased loaf pan (9" loaf pan).

Bake at 350° for 1 hour.
Yield: 1 loaf - recipe can be doubled. Check bread after about 50 minutes.

# Angel Biscuits
# Pat Bankhead

## Ingredients

5 Cups sifted self-rising flour
1 Teaspoon baking soda
3 tablespoons sugar
¾ Cup shortening
1 Package dry yeast dissolved in ½ cup warm (105-115°) water
2 Cups buttermilk

## Directions

Sift flour and measure.
Resift 3 times with soda and sugar.
Cut in shortening.
Soften yeast in water for 5 minutes.
Add yeast and buttermilk all at once.
Stir until moistened.
Roll out and cut . Bake 400 – 450° till done.
Dough will keep several days in covered container in refrigerator.

# Crème Brulée French Toast
## Betty Fontana

## Ingredients

½ Cup unsalted butter
1 Cup packed brown sugar
2 Tablespoons light corn syrup
1 Loaf of French, Italian or Country bread
5 eggs
1½ cups half-and-half
1 Teaspoon vanilla extract
1 Teaspoon (or a little more) of Grand Marnier
¼ Teaspoon salt

Melt the butter in a small saucepan over medium heat.

Add the brown sugar and corn syrup and cook until the mixture is smooth, stirring constantly.

Pour the mixture into a buttered 9x13 inch baking dish and spread evenly over the bottom.

Cut the bread into 1-inch thick slices, enough to fit in a single layer in the prepared baking dish.

Beat the eggs in a medium bowl.

Add the half-and-half, vanilla, Grand Marnier and salt mixture to the eggs and whisk until well blended.

Slowly pour the mixture evenly over the bread slices (bread will slowly absorb all the liquid).

Refrigerate, covered, for 8 hours to overnight.

Bring the baking dish to room temperature.

Bake uncovered, at 350° for 30 to 45 minutes or until golden brown.

Serve immediately by inverting the slices onto plates.

Yield 6 servings.

# Blueberry Bread
# Linda Williams

This delicious bread is almost like dessert. It is quick and easy and has become one of my favorites.

## Ingredients

1 Large egg
1 Cup milk
3 Tablespoons vegetable oil
2 Cups all-purpose flour
1 Cup sugar
2½ Teaspoons baking powder
½ Teaspoon salt
2 Cups fresh blueberries

## Directions

In a large bowl, beat the egg, milk and oil.

Combine the flour, sugar, baking powder and salt and gradually add to egg mixture, beating until combined.

Fold in blueberries.

Pour into a greased 9 x 5 in. loaf pan. Bake at 350º for 60-65 minutes or until a toothpick inserted near the center comes out clean.

Cool for 10 minutes before removing from pan to a wire rack to cool completely.

FREEZE OPTION: Securely wrap and freeze cooled loaf in plastic wrap and foil.

Thaw at room temperature to use.

# SOUPS

# SOUPS – TABLE OF CONTENTS

# Tomato-Cheese Soup
## Betty Adamson

## Ingredients

1 Can condensed tomato soup
1 Soup can milk or half and half
½ Cup sharp Cheddar cheese
¼ Teaspoon salt
1/8 Teaspoon pepper
3 Tablespoon dry sherry

## Directions

Heat all ingredients over low heat until
cheese melts.
Stir in Sherry.

# Taco Soup
## Daisy Serle

I made this soup for a work luncheon. Big mistake –
because I was asked to make it once a month for
years.

## Ingredients

1 Pound ground beef
1 Small onion diced
1 Small can green chilies
1 Can Rotel whole tomatoes
1 Can stewed tomatoes
1 Can sweet corn
1 Can great northern beans drained and
rinsed
1 Can pinto beans drained and rinsed
1 Can black beans drained and rinsed
1 Packet taco seasonings
1 Packet dry ranch dressing
4 Cups water

## Directions

Add ground beef to skillet and brown.
Drain.

Add onion to same skillet and brown.

In a large soup pot add all ingredients and simmer for 1 hour.

Serve over taco chips

I add shredded cheddar cheese on top of soup and sour cream.

# Italian Pasta Soup
## Daisy Serle

## Ingredients

1 Pound lean ground beef
2 Tablespoons olive oil – divided
1 Cup diced carrots
1 Cup diced celery
1 28-Ounce can tomato sauce
1 32-Ounce can chicken broth
1 28-Ounce can crushed tomatoes
1 28-Ounce can whole peeled plum tomatoes
2 Teaspoons granulated sugar
1½ Teaspoon dried basil
1 Teaspoon dried oregano
¾ Teaspoon dried thyme
Salt and fresh ground black pepper to taste
1 cup dry Ditalini pasta
1 (15-ounce) can garbanzo beans, drained and rinsed
1 (15-ounce) can great northern beans, drained and rinsed
Finely shredded Romano or Parmesan cheese, for serving

# Instructions

Heat 1 tablespoon olive oil in a large non-stick saucepan over medium heat, crumble in beef and cook, stirring occasionally until cooked through.

Add remaining 1 tablespoon olive oil and toss in carrots and celery over medium-high heat until tender (about 6 minutes).

Reduce heat to low, add tomato sauce, chicken broth, canned tomatoes, spices, and season with salt and pepper to taste.

Allow to simmer, stirring occasionally, until veggies are soft, about 20 minutes. Meanwhile, prepare pasta according to direction on package, cooking to al dente.

Add cooked and drained pasta to soup, along with beans. You can thin with some water if desired.

Serve with grated Romano or Parmesan cheese on top.

# Hamburger Soup
## Daisy Serle

## Ingredients

1 Pound lean ground beef
¼ Teaspoon pepper
¼ Teaspoon oregano
¼ Teaspoon basil
¼ Teaspoon seasoned salt
1 Envelope onion soup mix
3 Cups water
1 Can (8-ounces) tomato sauce
1 Tablespoon soy sauce
1 Cup sliced celery
1 Cup sliced carrots
1 Cup macaroni – cooked and drained
¼ Cup Parmesan cheese or cheddar cheese

## Directions

Crumble beef into slow cooker.

Add spices and soup mix.

Stir in water, tomato sauce and soy sauce; then add celery and carrots.

Cover and cook
on low for 6 to
8 hours.

Add cooked
macaroni and
Parmesan
cheese.

Cover and cook
on high for 10
to 15 minutes.

# Man's Hamburger Soup
## Anonymous

Fresh ginger gives this hearty pork meatball soup a
lively kick of flavor.

## Ingredients

1 Pound ground pork
2 Diced green onions
3 Cloves garlic – minced
1 Piece peeled grated fresh ginger
2 Quart lower-sodium chicken broth
8 Ounces snow peas
3 Cup Cooked white rice
½ Teaspoon salt
½ Teaspoon pepper

## Directions

Arrange oven rack 6 inches from broiler
heat source.

Preheat broiler on high.

Line large rimmed baking sheet with foil.

In medium bowl, combine pork, green onions, garlic, ginger, and pepper.

Form mixture into bite-size meatballs (about 1 inch each)

Arrange in single layer on prepared baking sheet. Broil 5 to 7 minutes, or until browned.

Meanwhile, in covered 5-quart saucepot, heat broth to simmering on high.

Uncover; add snow peas, rice, and broiled meatballs.

Reduce heat to medium; simmer 5 minutes, or until meatballs are cooked through and snow peas are tender.

# Easy Chicken Noodle Soup
## Pat Bankhead

## Ingredients

1 Tablespoon olive or vegetable oil
2 Cloves garlic – fine chopped
8 Medium green onions, sliced (½ cup)
(I use a medium yellow onion, diced)
2 Medium carrots – chopped (1 cup) (I use 4
or 5 cut on the diagonal)
3 Stalks celery, diced small
2 Cups cubed cooked chicken (I use a
rotisserie chicken, shredded)
2 Cups uncooked egg noodles (4 ounces)
(I use la Molisana brand from Publix)
1 Tablespoon chopped fresh parsley or 1
teaspoon parsley flakes
¼ Teaspoon pepper
1 dried bay leaf
5 ¼ Cups Progresso chicken broth (from 2-
32-Ounce cartons) May need more to get to
desired consistency

## Directions

In 3-quart saucepan, heat oil over medium
heat.

Add garlic, onions, celery and carrots: cook
4 minutes, stirring occasionally.

Stir in remaining ingredients. Heat to
Boiling, then reduce heat.

Cover: simmer about 10 minutes, until
carrots and noodles are tender.

Do not overcook noodles.

Remove bay leaf before serving.

# French-Market Onion Soup
## Betty Adamson

### Directions

1 Envelope onion-soup mix for 4 servings
French bread – sliced
1 8-Ounce Package Muenster cheese – shredded

### Directions

Heat soup mix and 4 cups water, stirring occasionally. Pour into individual casseroles.

Arrange a layer of the bread over soup; sprinkle with cheese. Repeat layers.

Bake at 450° until bubbly hot.

A great way to use up leftover bread!

# Broccoli-Cheese Soup
## Betty Adamson

## Ingredients

2 10-Ounce packages frozen broccoli cuts –
thawed
2 Cans cream of celery soup
2 Cup half and half
8-Ounce jar pasteurized process cheese
sauce
2 Cubes chicken bouillon
½ Tablespoon nutmeg
Salt and pepper to taste

## Directions

Mix All together, heat and serve.

# U.S. Senate Bean Soup
## Bobbie Herlong

## Ingredients

1½ Cups dry Great Northern beans
1 Smoked ham hock
1 Medium potato – finely diced
½ Cup diced celery
1 Clove garlic – minced
Salt and pepper to taste
Chopped parsley
1 Onion – diced
2 Quarts water

## Directions

Soak beans overnight in a quart of water.

Drain and measure two quarts liquid.

Combine beans, water and ham hock. Cover and simmer for 2 hours.

Let soup cool enough for any fat to accumulate and skim off, if necessary.

Remove ham hock, cut meat off bone and return meat to soup.

Add remaining ingredients. Add diced potato last so that it will not get too mushy. Cook 1 hour.

Remove 1 cup beans and 1 cup liquid and puree in blender or mash with potato masher.

Mix and serve hot.

# Corn Chowder
## Betty Adamson

## Ingredients

6 Bacon slices
1 Medium onion – thinly sliced
1 Can cream- style white corn
1½ Cups milk or half and half
1 Teaspoon salt
Dash pepper
2 Tablespoons chopped parsley

## Directions

Fry bacon until crisp, drain on paper towels
and break into large pieces.

Keep 2 tablespoons bacon drippings in
skillet, add onion and cook until tender.

Stir in corn, milk, salt and pepper. Garnish
with bacon and parsley.

# BON
# APPÉTIT